P9-DEZ-600

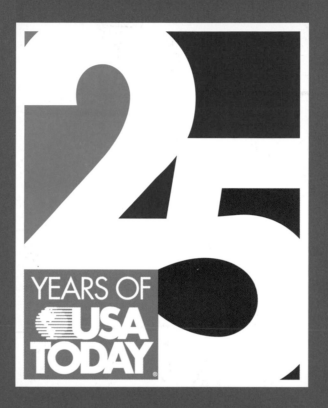

YEARS OF

USA
TODAY®

The Stories That Shape Our Nation

Copyright © USA TODAY, 2007

All rights reserved. Except for use in a review, no part of this publication may be reproduced, stored in or introduced into a retrieval system, or transmitted, in any form or by any means (electronic, mechanical, xerography, photocopy, recording or otherwise), without prior written permission of both the copyright owner and the publisher of this book. The scanning, uploading, and distribution of this book via the Internet or via any other means without the permission of the publisher is illegal and punishable by law.

FIRST EDITION

10 9 8 7 6 5 4 3 2 1

Library of Congress Cataloging-in-Publication Data available upon request

ISBN-10: 1-59670-287-7
ISBN-13: 978-1-59670-287-5

Spotlight Press, 804 North Neil Street, Champaign, Illinois 61820
Spotlight Press books are available for special promotions and premiums.

Publishers: Peter L. Bannon and Joseph J. Bannon Sr.
Senior managing editor: Susan M. Moyer
Project editor: Doug Hoepker
Art director: Dustin Hubbart
Acquisitions editor: Noah Adams Amstadter

A tribute in lights beams upward from next to Ground Zero in New York City on the second anniversary of the 9/11 attacks.
Robert Deutsch/USA TODAY

U.S. President Ronald Reagan and his Soviet counterpart Mikhail Gorbachev visit Governors Island in New York City on December 7, 1988. *Bill Swersey/AFP/Getty Images*

U.S. President Bill Clinton and Palestinian President Yasser Arafat stroll through the
White House's Rose Garden on April 20, 2000. *Mark Wilson/Newsmakers/Getty Images*

Lance Armstrong competes in stage 18 of the Tour de France on July 23, 1999.
Doug Pensinger/Getty Images

A person rides a donkey through a camp in South Darfur, Sudan, created to provide aid to people displaced by the genocide, May 2, 2005. *Jack Gruber/USA TODAY*

Penn State football head coach Joe Paterno (front, center) prepares to lead his team onto the field for a game on September 24, 2005. *Gregory Shamus/WireImage.com*

U.S. General H. Norman Schwarzkopf (front, center) speaks with soldiers of the 1st Infantry Division stationed in Saudi Arabia on January 13, 1991. *AP Images*

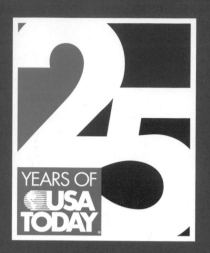

Part One
America's Headlines

Part Two
Global Headlines

Part Three
Trends and Changes

Part Four
25 Americans

Al Neuharth
AP Images

"USA TODAY hopes to serve as a forum for better understanding and unity to help make the USA truly one nation."

Al Neuharth
USA TODAY Founder

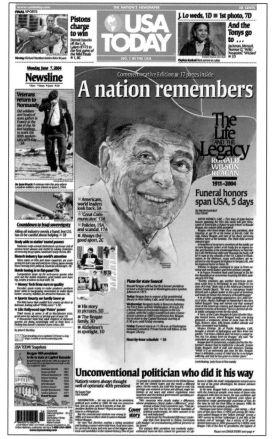

FOREWORD

On the night of the newspaper's birth in September 1982, USA TODAY Founder Al Neuharth had a question for me.

"So do you think it will sell?" Neuharth asked as he handed me a champagne glass.

Neuharth didn't know my name. The room was filled with dozens of young journalists like me who had come from all across the country to help launch this new national daily.

Ken Paulson
USA TODAY

I took a deep breath and answered, "I'm sure it will." Of course, I had no idea whether it would sell or not. At that moment in the kick-off celebration, there really didn't seem to be any other appropriate answer.

Twenty-five years later, it's hard to say which was less likely: that USA TODAY would indeed sell in such record numbers that it would became the top newspaper in America, or that the nervous young staffer would end up being its editor.

This book celebrates the anniversary of "The Nation's Newspaper" and salutes the spirit of America that made it possible.

From the outset, USA TODAY was a decidedly different newspaper. We knew that Americans were strapped for time, so we condensed our stories and didn't jump them from page to page. We knew that television was our main rival, so we revved up the visuals and splashed our pages with color.

We also set a different goal for a different kind of newspaper. Our mission statement — written by Neuharth — appeared atop the editorial page on our first day of publication and has been there ever since:

"USA TODAY hopes to serve as a forum for better understanding and unity to help make the USA truly one nation."

That wasn't marketing. That was the gut feeling of a man with humble roots in rural South Dakota who took full advantage of everything America had to offer.

"Truly one nation" meant putting together a newsroom with staffers from all over this country, young and old, of many races and faiths, all reflecting the rich diversity of this nation. That first generation of USA TODAY staffers was less experienced than some of their big media counterparts, but it was also less cynical. That meant a fresh perspective that would set us apart from the pack.

Neuharth, whose remarks and writings are often laden with alliterations and internal rhymes, said that his newspaper would report "the good and bad, the glad and the sad." Corny? Sure. Simplistic? No doubt. But it was also a pure distillation of why this newspaper would be different.

This collection of USA TODAY stories and photos celebrates the successes and chronicles the crises of the nation's past quarter century.

Al Neuharth (in white jacket on right) and Ken Paulson (in brown-and-white striped tie) celebrate the printing of the first edition of USA TODAY on September 15, 1982. *USA TODAY*

Much has changed in that time. Eight-tracks have given way to iPods. MTV has been eclipsed by YouTube. And the news industry, once limited to print and broadcast media, now informs the public through an unprecedented array of products and platforms. For our part, USA TODAY has expanded from the newspaper to USATODAY.com, USAT TODAY Live, USA TODAY Sports Weekly, USA Weekend and even a version of USA TODAY for your cell phone.

What hasn't changed is our core mission: reporting fully and fairly on the events of our time. This book captures the extraordinary moments of the past 25 years, from the inspiration of the Olympics to the devastation of 9/11; from the fall of the Berlin Wall to the rise of the Internet.

Among the other stirring stories of the past 25 years:

▸ The tragic loss of the brave crews of two space shuttles.

▸ The meltdown of the stock market in 1987, giving all of us just a taste of what our grandparents saw in 1929.

▸ The polarizing verdict in the O.J. Simpson murder trial.

▸ The 1998 race for the home run title that invigorated baseball and set the stage for scandals to come.

▸ The most unexpected presidential election of all as the U.S. Supreme Court cast the final votes.

▸ The faint stirrings of liberty in China and the showdown in Tiananmen Square.

▸ The devastating tsunami in Asia that took more than 200,000 lives.

▸ The death of Princess Diana.

▸ The impeachment of a president.

▸ The horrific act of domestic terrorism in Oklahoma City.

▸ Two wars with Iraq with strikingly different results.

All of these stories riveted the nation. Some brought us together. Others divided us. But throughout our history at USA TODAY, we've seen time and again how much Americans truly share.

I'm reminded of that every time I sit down next to a stranger on an airplane and happen to strike up a conversation. It doesn't take long for most Americans to find common ground. We care about the big game. We're still talking about what we saw last night on the hot television show. And by and large we care deeply about where this nation is headed.

It's the water cooler conversation writ large. And of course, those shared interests and values are what make a national newspaper possible.

This is truly one nation. And we're honored to play our part.

Ken Paulson

Ken Paulson
Editor of USA TODAY

PART ONE
AMERICA'S HEADLINES

1986–1987

IRAN-CONTRA AFFAIR

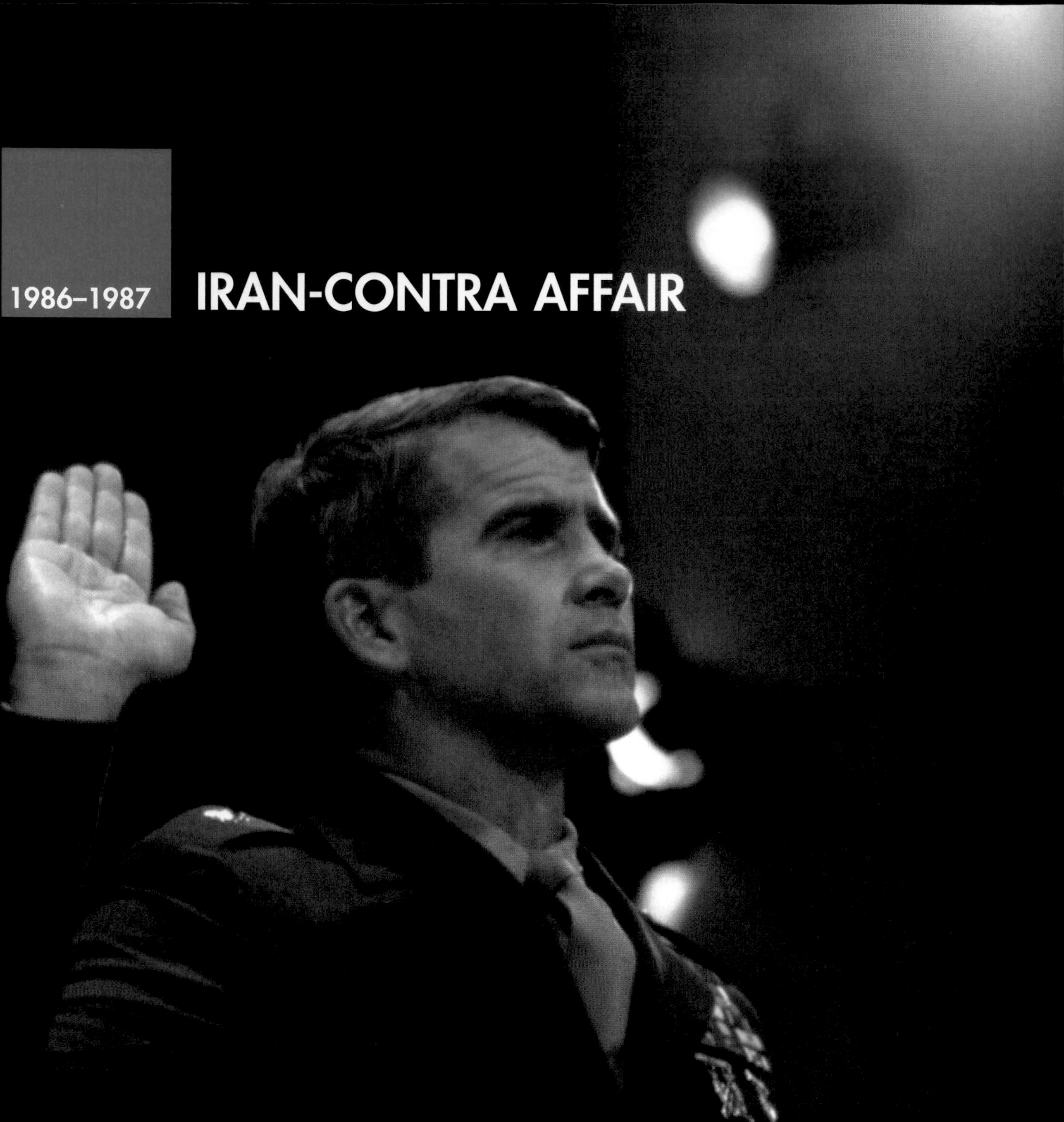

"It's a bipartisan hurricane"

By Johanna Neuman
Excerpt from article published November 26, 1986

WASHINGTON — A firestorm of protest greeted Tuesday's White House admission it was secretly funneling money from Iranian arms merchants to Nicaraguan rebels.

"It was a bipartisan storm," Sen. Carl Levin, D-Mich., said of last week's credibility crisis over the arms-for-hostages deal with Iran. "Now it's a bipartisan hurricane."

Sen. David Durenberger, R-Minn., said, "I don't know who knew what was going on, but . . . it will be a cold day in Washington, D.C., before any more money goes into Nicaragua." . . .

Other reaction:

▸ "It was a shocking revelation and it further shows up the chaotic state of our foreign policy," said Senate Democratic leader Robert Byrd, D-W.Va. "The president does not know what is going on in the basement of the White House."

▸ Senate Republican leader Robert Dole, R-Kan., called it "a bizarre twist" and urged caution before "final judgments are drawn." . . . ■

After two reports, Iran-Contra picture is still blurred

By Leslie Phillips
November 19, 1987

Despite the Congress and the presidential Tower Commission, questions remain.

"Still the record is incomplete," said House panel Chairman Rep. Lee Hamilton, D-Ind.

Some causes cited:

The death of CIA Director William Casey, shredded documents, and the faulty memory of witnesses (Attorney General Edwin Meese testified "I do not recall" 340 times).

Still unknown:

▸ Whose idea was the diversion? Lt. Col.

Oliver North testified middleman Manucher Ghorbanifar suggested the idea to him in a London men's room in early 1986. But, according to Israeli documents, North told an Israeli Ministry of Defense official about the diversion plot as early as December 1985.

▸ Whose money was used in the diversion? The majority report concludes the money belongs to the U.S. Treasury. The minority report says it may well belong to Richard Secord and Albert Hakim.

▸ Were laws broken? It's left to special prosecutor Lawrence Walsh and the courts. ■

Lt. Col. Oliver North, the central figure in the Iran-Contra affair, prepares to testify before Congress. North was the architect of the scheme that sent arms to Iran in exchange for money and possibly the release of hostages. The money was then sent — illegally — to the contras in Nicaragua, a right-wing organization that was battling Nicaragua's leftist government. *Tim Dillon/USA TODAY*

BLACK MONDAY

Main street fidgets as Wall St. burns

By Kevin Maney, Harriet C. Johnson and Pam Yip
Excerpt from article published October 20, 1987

Doom swallowed Wall Street Monday. Bad news was expected, but the crash reached a scale nobody could have imagined.

By Monday's close, the Dow sank below 1739, wiping out a half trillion dollars in stocks' market value, as measured by a broader index of more than 5,000 issues. Only 108 stocks survived the debacle that posted 1,973 declines.

Sam Walton, identified by *Forbes* magazine as the USA's richest man, expressed concern for shareholders in his Wal-Mart Stores when he heard the news. But his own loss — $1 billion plus — he took in stride: "It's paper anyway. It was paper when we started and it's paper afterward."

October 20, 1987

After a day of frantic deals and jammed computers and phone lines, thousands of dazed traders wandered Wall Street — closed to traffic Monday — to trade grim jokes and theories about what went wrong.

"Everyone is going bananas," said James Hunter, 25, a trader for Dean Witter Reynolds.

Tourists flocked to the New York Stock Exchange gothic headquarters in lower Manhattan. "They want to see the stock market crash," said a messenger named Dominic.

The panic even reached overseas, tumbling stocks in London, Tokyo and other foreign exchanges.

For the high-stakes set, the worst day in stock market history marked the end of five years of fireworks and windfalls. "Last week I said the world wasn't coming to an end. Now I'm not sure," said Hugh Johnson of First Albany Corp.

But elsewhere in the USA, away from trading floors and millionaires, the panic was tempered by disbelief. Many decided not to panic, but to hold onto their stocks.

"At the moment, there's an overreaction," said Dr. Scheldon Kress, 56, a Potomac, Md. physician who plans to hold his stock. In Cincinnati, stock investor Scott Bowles, 78, said, "The people who are panicked are all the jerks on Wall Street who all try to go through the gate at once."

The crash clearly caused anxiety and concern, however, among investors, brokers and financial planners within sight of a stock ticker. In many homes, the fate of family stocks became dinner-table conversation.

Small investors tried to analyze whether the crash means impending economic disaster or a much-needed correction.

Experts expected the market to open on a down note Monday. Last Friday, the Dow lost 108 points — at the time, a seeming catastrophe. The fall started Oct. 5 because of fears of rising interest rates and renewed inflation, plus soured investor psychology. But now, the market gains of an entire year are wiped out. The losses easily mark this as a bear market.

Most of the big sellers — and big losers — were institutions, such as pension funds. But, said Norm Zadeh, who runs a real-money stock trading contest from Beverly Hills, Calif.: "It's not just a few people losing, it's the whole country losing." . . . ∎

A trader on the New York Stock Exchange reacts as stock prices plummet on October 19, 1987, which came to be known as "Black Monday." It took until January of 1989 for the Dow Jones to return to a pre-crash average.
Maria R. Bastone/AFP/ Getty Images

SAN FRANCISCO BAY EARTHQUAKE 1989

A collapsed section of the Bay Bridge, October 17, 1989. The bridge reopened on November 16. *Chuck Nacke/Time Life Pictures/ Getty Images*

A collapsed house sits on a crushed car parked in the Marina District. The earthquake left 13,000 people homeless.
Adam Teitelbaum/AFP/ Getty Images

Killer quake jolts the Bay Area

By Judy Keen
October 18, 1989

A violent earthquake shuddered through northern California Tuesday during rush hour, killing at least 200 in the San Francisco area.

The quake terrified 60,000 World Series fans in Candlestick Park, who screamed as the stadium swayed. The game was postponed.

Today is critical: There's a chance of an even larger quake in the first 24 hours after a major temblor. Five strong aftershocks hit Tuesday night.

Experts say the area should brace for landslides and fires.

"It felt like one of those huge monsters from a Japanese horror movie grabbed a hold of the building and was shaking the hell out of it," said Margie Cornehl, a San Jose employee.

ABC baseball announcer Al Michaels was on the air as the quake hit. "I'll tell you what, we're having an earth-," he said before power was lost. Networks dumped prime-time programs to provide coverage.

California officials report people died on Interstate 880 in Oakland; in a Santa Cruz shopping mall; in the collapse of a San Francisco apartment building; and on the Bay Bridge after a 30-foot section of the upper deck caved in.

The quake registered 6.9 on the Richter scale — a major quake — and the worst since the 1906 San Francisco earthquake, estimated at 8.3.

The quake was the continental USA's worst since 1952.

The Richter scale measures ground motion; each one-digit increase means a tenfold increase in magnitude.

The quake's center was on a segment of the

San Andreas Fault where stress had built up, says Lisa Wald, a U.S. Geological Survey seismologist.

Tremors were felt 800 miles away in Los Angeles. Damage was nightmarish:

▸ Fire blazed in San Francisco's Marina District and on the campus of the University of California at Berkeley.

▸ Most of the bridges connecting San Francisco to its suburbs were closed for inspection; the famous Golden Gate Bridge was undamaged.

▸ Up to 1 million customers lost electricity. Gas and phone service were also cut.

▸ Buildings and the Highway 101 bridge collapsed in Hollister.

▸ The Diablo Canyon nuclear plant on the San Andreas fault near San Francisco is on alert to check for damage.

Officials wasted no time:

▸ California's National Guard has been activated.

▸ "We're taking care of one another. . . . There's no disaster," said San Francisco Mayor Art Agnos.

▸ California Gov. William Deukmejian cut short a trade mission to Frankfurt, West Germany.

▸ The White House sent Transportation Secretary Samuel Skinner and Vice President Quayle, already in California. ■

ABOVE: Will Clark of the San Francisco Giants and his son walk across the field after the earthquake struck, postponing the third game of the 1989 World Series between the Giants and another Bay Area team, the Oakland Athletics. *Otto Greule Jr./Getty Images*

LEFT: Claire Isaacs carries a sign through section 53 at Candlestick Park, October 27, 1989, prior to the restart of the earthquake-delayed World Series. After play continued, the Giants were swept by the Athletics. *AP Images*

Collapsed houses in the Marina District. Sixty-seven people died in the quake, including four in the Marina District. *Otto Greule Jr./Getty Images*

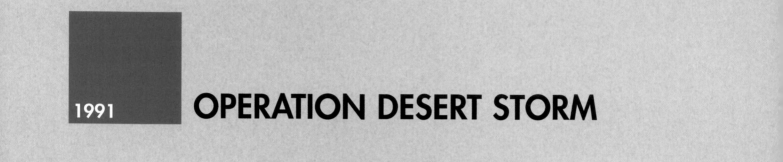

1991 **OPERATION DESERT STORM**

Iraqi soldiers cross a highway carrying white surren-
der flags, February 25, 1991. Tens of thousands of Iraqi
troops surrendered to the United States and its allies.
Christophe Simon/AFP/Getty Images

Freed Kuwaitis shower troops with gratitude

By Kirk Spitzer
February 28, 1991

KUWAIT CITY — On their first full day of freedom from Iraqi occupation, Kuwaitis exploded Wednesday in an outpouring of joy, mobbing allied troops in delirious gratitude.

The cheering Kuwaitis honked horns, waved Kuwaiti and American flags, chanted "USA, USA" and showered troops with affection unseen since GIs liberated western Europe in World War II.

They threw candy, cigarettes and Kuwaiti flags at the Marines and begged for American flags.

In every window, they blew kisses, waved, flashed V-for-victory signs or shouted "We love you" and "Thank you."

For one convoy of Marine combat vehicles, what was supposed to be a simple tour of the battered city turned into a triumphal liberation parade.

"I never expected that," said Lt. Gen. Walter Boomer, the Marine commander. "I thought, what a great thing America has done to see the joy on their faces. I'll keep that memory forever."

"You couldn't pay for this," said Sgt. Anthony Tavarone, 23, of Lake Place, Fla.

Hundreds of Kuwaitis gathered Wednesday near the U.S. Embassy in celebration, and mobbed the convoy.

When Marines emerged to unsnarl the traffic jam, those in the crowd shook their hands, coaxed them to pose for pictures and asked them to sign diaries carried by children.

Even reporters were pulled from vehicles and kissed on the cheeks by Kuwaiti men.

"Bush is great. America is great. You tell them," said a man who identified himself only as Ahmed. ∎

January 19-20, 1991

U.S. Marine Corporal Matt Robbins holds a Kuwaiti boy celebrating the ouster of occupying Iraqi troops, February 27, 1991. *Todd Buchanan/Time Life Pictures/Getty Images*

TOP: U.S. President George H. W. Bush and the Chairman of the Joint Chiefs of Staff, General Colin Powell, May 23, 1991. The war led to the "Powell doctrine," which called for overwhelming force, solid domestic support and a clear exit strategy for war. *Diana Walker/Time Life Pictures/Getty Images*

BELOW: U.S. General H. Norman Schwarzkopf is shown at ease standing in front of a tank in Saudi Arabia, January 12, 1991. "Stormin' Norman" commanded the allied forces in the Gulf War. *AP Images*

OPPOSITE: Oil fires burn in Kuwait, July 1, 1991. *Robert Deutsch/USA TODAY*

U.S. forces cross a desert heavily marked by tire treads during the Gulf War.
Win McNamee/Department of Defense/Time Life Pictures/Getty Images

RIOTING IN LOS ANGELES

Tensions explode in L.A.

By Sally Ann Stewart and Haya El Nasser

Excerpt from article published April 30, 1992

ABOVE: Video of the police beating of Rodney King was filmed by pedestrian George Holliday. Once released to the public, the footage created a firestorm of controversy in America. *USA TODAY*

OPPOSITE: Structures burn and smoulder along Vermont Avenue in Los Angeles, April 30, 1992. Rioting was sparked by the acquittal of four white policemen accused in the beating of Rodney King. For three days, Vermont Avenue was a thoroughfare for gunmen, arsonists and looters who torched its buildings and terrorized residents. *AP Images*

LOS ANGELES — Less than three hours after acquittal verdicts for four Los Angeles police officers, gangs of youths took to the streets in search of their own brand of justice.

They looted stores, attacked passing cars and trucks and set fires — first in south-central Los Angeles, later downtown.

Officials described it as the city's worst rioting since the 1965 outbreak in Watts that lasted six days and left 34 dead.

Some drivers, trying to avoid flying rocks and bottles, crashed into each other, then ran to nearby businesses.

But businesses weren't safe, either. A corner liquor store and gas station were looted.

Local television showed several youths pulling a truck driver from his cab and beating him with crowbars. One youth spit on him, another smashed a heavy object on his head.

Live helicopter shots showed no police on the scene. . . . ■

Los Angeles police form a line to prevent a crowd from looting a store, April 30, 1992.
AP Images

The Alfred P. Murrah Federal Building in Oklahoma City on April 20, 1995, the day after the explosion. The bombing killed 168 people. *Brad Markel/Getty Images*

OKLAHOMA CITY
BOMBING
1995

An unidentified woman comforts an injured child, April 19, 1995, outside the Alfred P. Murrah Federal Building . A day-care center was located in the building. *AP Images*

Hunt for "killers" — and survivors

By David Craig and Steve Marshall
April 20, 1995

OKLAHOMA CITY — A huge bomb blast Wednesday shredded half of a federal building here and most of whatever sense of security remains in America's heartland.

"It was an act of cowardice and it was evil," said President Clinton. "These people are killers and they must be treated like killers."

The explosion, at 9 a.m. CT, is being called the worst act of terrorism on U.S. soil, killing dozens, injuring hundreds and leaving at least 250 missing.

The car bomb blasted away an entire side of the nine-story building, raining glass shards over six city blocks and was felt at least 30 miles away.

"It was like Beirut, everything was burning," said physician Carl Spengler, who arrived minutes after the blast.

A massive FBI investigation began immediately, with teams of agents being flown in.

"We will find the perpetrators and bring them to justice," vowed Attorney General Janet Reno. "The death penalty is available and we will seek it."

The loss of life was heightened by casualties from a second-floor daycare center, with at least 12 children killed.

"The daycare center is totally gone," said Spengler. "At the time it blew up, the place should have been full."

Andy Sullivan, a Children's Hospital surgeon, crawled through basement rubble to perform an on-site amputation. He removed the right leg of a woman trapped under a beam.

Search and rescue teams flew in from Sacramento and Phoenix. "We just hope there are some people . . . surviving," said Oklahoma City deputy fire chief Jon Hansen.

Rescuers have "to crawl over corpses" to get to survivors.

A light drizzle turned into a downpour, hampering rescue efforts. "We may be here the next three days getting heavy equipment in," said Hansen. ■

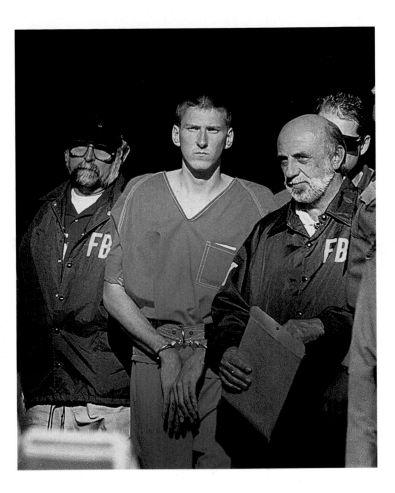

ABOVE: Timothy McVeigh, in handcuffs, saw the bombing as a "military operation" against the United States government, according to his attorney. He was found guilty and executed July 11, 2001. *Robert Hanashiro/USA TODAY*

LEFT: Justin Flagg, 7, and his father pause to reflect on May 2, 1995, at the federal building. The Flagg family came to Oklahoma City to bring 4,000 teddy bears they collected as a gesture of solidarity with survivors and people affected by the explosion. *Roberto Schmidt/AFP/Getty Images*

O.J. SIMPSON TRIAL

Acquittal triggers day of anger, joy

By Richard Price and Sally Ann Stewart
Excerpt from article published October 4, 1995

LOS ANGELES — O.J. Simpson, acquitted of double-murder charges, celebrated his freedom with a party at his estate Tuesday while outside several hundred people chanted "Guilty, guilty, guilty."

The contrast of emotions spread from the courtroom across the nation when the "not guilty" verdicts were read by Judge Lance Ito's clerk after a marathon nine-month trial.

Simpson mouthed the words "thank you" to the jury. His family members rejoiced, while the families of victims Nicole Brown Simpson and Ronald Goldman were in tears.

Afterward, Simpson's mother, Eunice, told the media: "I was always in prayer. I knew that my son was innocent."

Separately, an agonized Fred Goldman, father of Ron Goldman, said, "The prosecution team didn't lose today. I deeply believe that this country lost today."

One prosecutor, Christopher Darden, burst into tears as he spoke to the media.

Simpson's lawyers may have been victorious, but defense lawyer Robert Shapiro provided insights about disagreements on the team.

He told ABC he fought lead lawyer Johnnie Cochran's decision to use race as an issue. "Not only did we play the race card, we dealt it from the bottom of the deck." ...

The jury of nine blacks, two whites and one Hispanic reached its verdict Monday in less than four hours. Said juror Brenda Moran: "I think we did the right thing. As a matter of fact, I know we did."

In a scene reminiscent of the slow-speed Bronco chase last year, Simpson was taken to his estate Tuesday in a white van while news helicopters tracked him overhead.

Los Angeles Police Chief Willie Williams said he had no plans to reopen the probe.

But Simpson, in a statement read by son Jason, vowed to track down the killers who are "out there somewhere." ◼

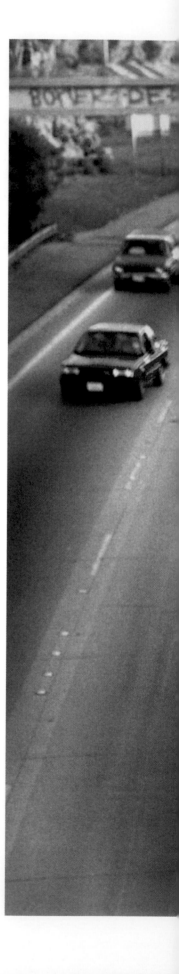

A white Ford Bronco, driven by Al Cowlings and carrying O.J. Simpson, is trailed by police cars on a southern California freeway on June 17, 1994. The slow-speed chase was shown live on TV. *AP Images*

"If it doesn't fit, you must acquit," attorney Johnnie Cochran told the jury. The gloves Simpson tried on in the courtroom on June 21, 1995 were the same size as a pair found at the murder scene. According to Cochran, that the gloves didn't fit proved someone else committed the murder. *Vince Bucci/AFP/Getty Images*

Simpson Trial Record

The Simpson trial was not California's longest murder trial (the Hillside Strangler lasted two years), but passed the Charles Manson trial as longest with a sequestered jury.

Trial facts:

▸ Days O.J. Simpson jailed: 474

▸ Days since jury selection began: 372

▸ Trial/investigation cost to county: $9 million

▸ Days jury sequestered: 266

▸ Testimony days: 133 (prosecution 99, defense 34)

▸ Witnesses: 126 (prosecution 72, defense 54)

▸ Exhibits: 857 (prosecution 488, defense 369)

CLEVELAND RAINS ON BOSTON; N.Y. SINKS SEATTLE 9-6

- COLORADO CAN'T CAPITALIZE ON BASES-LOADED 9th; ATLANTA WINS 5-4
- CINCINNATI GETS 4 IN THE FIRST, POUNDS L.A. 7-2
- BASEBALL, 1,4-7C

Frank Becerra Jr., Gannett Suburban
HOME RUN: Randy Velarde, Wade Boggs celebrate, **1C**

USA TODAY

NO. 1 IN THE USA . . . FIRST IN DAILY READERS

POPE ARRIVES FOR 4TH U.S. TRIP TONIGHT

U.N. SPEECH, MASSES IN N.Y., N.J., MD., ON HIS AGENDA, **9A**

COUNTRY MUSIC AWARDS HEAVY ON PERFORMANCES

VINCE GILL TO HOST SHOW FEATURING 21 FULL SONGS; TONIGHT AT 8 ET ON CBS, **1D**
- LINEUP AND BALLOT, **7D**

Robert Deutsch, USA TODAY
SHANIA TWAIN: Hot new artist will sing, **1D**

WEDNESDAY

SIMPSON FREE

WEDNESDAY, OCTOBER 4, 1995

NEWSLINE

A QUICK READ ON THE NEWS

WALL STREET: Dow Jones industrial average falls 11.56 points to 4749.70; Nasdaq index drops 7.12 to 1020.45; 30-year Treasury bond yield sinks to 6.45%. 1,4B.

AFFIRMATIVE ACTION: Congressional Republicans drop affirmative action from legislative agenda; measures limiting preference programs are not likely to be voted on this year. 12A.

CHRYSLER 'MUDSLINGING': Dissident shareholder Kirk Kerkorian and former Chrysler financial chief are "trashing" company, says Chrysler CEO Robert Eaton; two say they're "monitoring our investment." 1B.

HUMAN TESTS: Probe, launched by Energy Secretary Hazel O'Leary, left, into secret Cold War program conducting radiation experiments on thousands of unwitting Americans, ends after two years of sifting through millions of once-classified files; President Clinton apologizes to victims, orders review of research involving human subjects. 10A.

AP
O'LEARY: 'Story . . . has many pieces'

HURRICANE: Opal strengthens, zeros in on northeast Gulf Coast with 115-mph winds; landfall expected today on Florida's panhandle. Hurricane warnings posted from Alabama east. 10A.

CLINTON VETO: President Clinton issues third veto while in office, nixing a bill paying costs of running Congress, citing lack of work on federal spending bills. 12A.

NFL FINES: Pittsburgh coach, officials fined for tiff, bad call; AFC team-by-team statistics. NFL. 1, 8-10,12C.

EDITORIAL: O.J. Simpson trial verdict. In USA TODAY's opinion, "While the verdict ended the trial, it didn't begin to end the story. Too many compelling subplots remain incomplete." 14A.

MONEY: Economy is worse than most experts may think, says manager of $53 billion Magellan Fund. 1B.
- Third-quarter stock mutual fund results. 3B.

SPORTS: Trades in NHL; one involves 3 teams. 1,16C.
- David Clark, 70, solo skipper, occasional clarinet player for tips in trip around the world, says farewell to his boat Sea Me Now after violent storm. Sailing Diary. 12C.

LIFE: Folic acid, B vitamin recommended to pregnant women to reduce spinal birth defects, could prevent up to 50,000 heart disease deaths a year, say researchers. 1D.
- 96-year-old New York law professor teaches law and laughs; dog teaches kids old books. Education Today. 4-5D.

COMING TOMORROW

BOOK BATTLES: Michael Crichton's new novel competes with Colin Powell's autobiography in the complete list of USA's 50 best sellers.

By John O. Buckley

Inside USA TODAY 4 SECTIONS

Crossword	8D
Editorial/Opinion	14-15A
Lotteries	7D
Marketplace Today	7-8D
State-by-state	11A
Stocks	4,6-9B

© COPYRIGHT 1995 USA TODAY, a division of Gannett Co., Inc.

USA SNAPSHOTS®

---

12 PAGES OF COVERAGE

Pool photo by Myung J. Chun
RELIEF: Johnnie Cochran hugs O.J. Simpson after televised verdict is read. Even President Clinton watched.

Pool photo by David Sprague
DISTRAUGHT: Fred Goldman, father of victim Ronald Goldman, with wife Patti by his side.

Goldman family's 'nightmare' began with murder and ends with dreadful disbelief, 4A

Pool photo by Myung J. Chun
THANKFUL: Eunice Simpson, mother of O.J. Simpson, clasps her hands as verdict is read.

Simpson family celebrates at home after ride on 'emotional roller coaster' is over, 4A

- USA's reaction to verdict often depends on race, **6A**; index, **3A**
- Workplace came to a halt, costing employers billions, **1B**
- What is the link, if any, between sports and domestic violence? **1C**
- TV circus undermined whatever value courtroom cameras had, **1D**

COVER STORY

Prosecutors 'ran from their evidence'

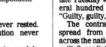

USA TODAY / CNN GALLUP POLL

What would the verdict have been if Simpson were . . .

White

Guilty	41%
Not guilty	45%

NEWS ANALYSIS

By Tony Mauro
Legal Affairs Correspondent
USA TODAY

The defense never rested. And the prosecution never woke up.

In the search to explain Tuesday's verdict in the trial of the century, what emerges

---

Acquittal triggers day of anger, joy

By Richard Price and Sally Ann Stewart
USA TODAY

LOS ANGELES — O.J. Simpson, acquitted of double-murder charges, celebrated his freedom with a party at his estate Tuesday while outside several hundred people chanted "Guilty, guilty, guilty."

The contrast of emotions spread from the courtroom across the nation when the "not guilty" verdicts were read by Judge Lance Ito's clerk after a marathon nine-month trial.

concerns the future of the Simpson children, Justin, 7, and Sydney, 9.

Nicole Simpson's family likely will have to give up custody because Simpson agreed to it only until he was able to resume custody.

They told ABC late Tuesday that the children have been told that "Daddy's free."

Nicole's father, Lou Brown, said, "We're still in a wonderment area. . . . We gain nothing in fighting" for custody.

Simpson also faces three

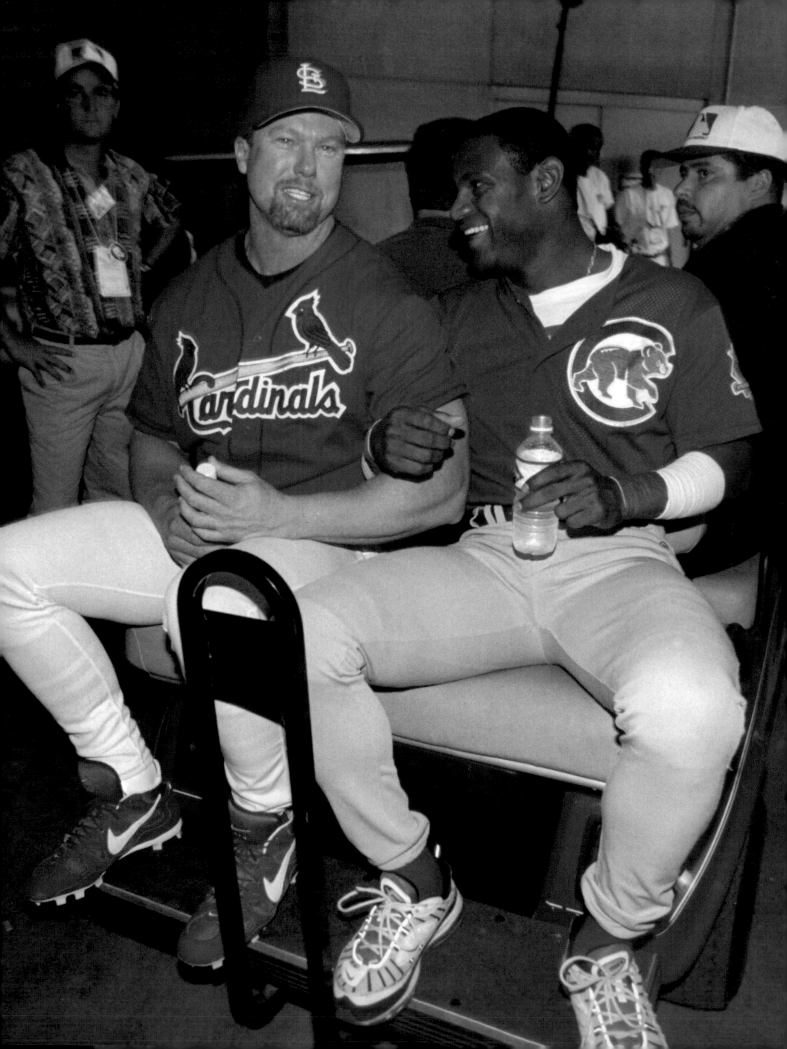

Blasting away the past

By Mel Antonen
September 9, 1998

ST. LOUIS — Mark McGwire on Tuesday kissed the bat Roger Maris used to hit his 61st homer in 1961. Three hours later, he kissed Maris' home-run record goodbye.

The St. Louis Cardinals first baseman became the first player in baseball history to reach 62 home runs in a season when he hit an atypical McGwire home run in a 6-3 win against the Chicago Cubs.

The history-making home run came in his second at-bat, in the fourth, against starter Steve Trachsel — a low-flying line drive that disappeared over the left-field fence in Busch Stadium.

It traveled an estimated 341 feet, McGwire's shortest home run this season by 6 feet.

OPPOSITE: Mark McGwire of the St. Louis Cardinals and Sammy Sosa of the Chicago Cubs leave a joint press conference at Busch Stadium in St. Louis, Missouri, on September 7, 1998. McGwire and Sosa traded the home-run lead over the course of the summer before McGwire finally pulled ahead.
Vincent Laforet/Getty Images

ABOVE: The Busch Stadium scoreboard shows the final home-run tally.
Robert Hanashiro/USA TODAY

House members take swings

By Chris Jenkins
Excerpt from article published March 18, 2005

WASHINGTON — Members of a congressional committee swung away at Major League Baseball on Thursday during more than 11 hours of hearings on steroid use in the game.

Doctors, parents, lawyers, MLB officials and six current or former players were brought before the House Government Reform Committee, fielding questions on subjects ranging from steroids in society to baseball's new testing procedure.

"Players that are guilty of taking steroids are not only cheaters — you are cowards," said Donald Hooton of Plano, Texas, whose 17-year-old son killed himself in July 2003 after taking steroids.

Retired slugger Mark McGwire repeatedly refused to join three other players in denying use of performance-enhancing drugs. He became emotional when talking about the testimony from parents whose sons had killed themselves.

Responding to occasional aggressive questioning from committee members, McGwire said repeatedly he "wasn't here to talk about the past."

He was not, however, pressured by committee members to the point that he had to plead the Fifth Amendment, which forbids forcing witnesses to testify against themselves. . . . ■

ia Rosell   Mr. Mark McGwire   Mr. Rafael Palmeiro

Left to right: Jose Canseco, attorney Jim Sharp, Sammy Sosa, interpreter Patricia Rosell, Mark McGwire, Rafael Palmeiro and Curt Schilling testify before Congress on March 17, 2005, during a hearing on steroid use in Major League Baseball. Palmeiro told the lawmakers he had never used steroids, but tested positive later in the year.
Tim Dillon/USA TODAY

Clinton issues angry denial

By Bill Nichols and Kevin Johnson
Excerpt from article published January 27, 1998

WASHINGTON — President Clinton issued on Monday his most forceful denial of allegations that he had an affair with former White House intern Monica Lewinsky and urged her to lie about it.

"I did not have sexual relations with that woman, Miss Lewinsky," Clinton said at the end of a White House event to highlight a child-care proposal. "I never told anybody to lie. Not a single time. Never. These allegations are false. And I need to go back to work for the American people."

But Lewinsky's lawyer, William Ginsburg, said Monday night that he had given a formal outline, known as a proffer, to Whitewater independent counsel Kenneth Starr about what she would testify to in exchange for immunity.

People familiar with Starr's negotiations said that to receive immunity, Lewinsky must admit to having sex with Clinton, which she denied in an earlier affidavit, as well as discuss any cover-up efforts. . . .

Clinton's statement, delivered with first lady Hillary Rodham Clinton at his side, showed a new White House resolve to deny any affair and cover-up and essentially dare Starr to prove otherwise. . . . ■

ABOVE: Monica Lewinsky smiles during an interview with USA TODAY in December of 1999, almost two years after she first entered the headlines. "I just need to try to be a normal 26 year old," she said.
Robert Hanashiro/USA TODAY

OPPOSITE: President Clinton strongly denies any sexual relationship with Monica Lewinsky in a statement made in the Roosevelt Room of the White House on January 26, 1998.
Tim Dillon/USA TODAY

ABOVE: The Clintons — Hillary, Chelsea, Bill and dog Buddy — depart from the South Lawn of the White House on August 18, 1998. It was their first public appearance since the President admitted having a relationship with Lewinsky. *Tim Dillon/USA TODAY*

RIGHT: A truck passes crowds of Super Bowl fans in San Diego for Super Bowl XXXII with a sign calling for President Bill Clinton's impeachment. *Julia Schmalz/USA TODAY*

Debate, defiance, decision

By Kathy Kiely
Excerpt from article published December 21, 1998

For the elected representatives of the world's greatest power, meeting amid an armed conflict to perform one of their most solemn constitutional duties, the battle was fiercely partisan and intensely personal.

Was the argument about sex, or equal justice under the law? Was the nation at war with Iraq, or were its representatives at war with each other? During a long weekend of slamming gavels, bitter accusations and sordid revelations, it sometimes was difficult to tell.

Eleven months after independent counsel Ken Starr launched his investigation into President Clinton's alleged efforts to cover up an affair with former White House intern Monica Lewinsky, the high drama of constitutional conflict mingled with the low whispers of sexual secrets in the U.S. Capitol.

Meeting in a rare, lame-duck session and voting on almost straight party lines, the lawmakers voted to impeach a president for only the second time in history just days after endorsing his bombing raids on Iraq.

After a marathon, 13-hour debate Friday, the lawmakers approved two articles of impeachment Saturday. An article accusing Clinton of perjury before a grand jury passed on a 228-206 vote. Another, which alleges the president obstructed justice in the sex harassment case that former Arkansas state employee Paula Jones filed against him, passed 221-212.

Two articles were rejected: One accusing Clinton of perjury in a deposition he gave to Jones' lawyers on a 229-205 vote; the other contending he abused his office in attempting to conceal the Lewinsky affair, 285-148.... ∎

House Judiciary Committee Chairman Henry Hyde (center, white hair) is surrounded during a discussion during the Clinton impeachment hearings on December 10, 1998. *Tim Dillon/USA TODAY*

IN COLUMBINE'S WAKE

March 22, 2005

Before killing himself, Jeff Weise, 16, fatally shoots five schoolmates, a teacher, and an unarmed guard on March 21, 2005, at Red Lake High School on the Red Lake Indian Reservation in Minnesota.

October 3, 2006

Charles Roberts IV, a milk truck driver, takes hostages on Oct. 2, 2006, at West Nickel Mines School, an Amish schoolhouse in Lancaster County, Pennsylvania. He kills five girls, wounds five others, then kills himself.

April 17, 2007

In the deadliest U.S. school massacre, Seung Hui Cho, a student at Virginia Tech, kills 32 people on April 16, 2007, in shootings at two locations on campus in Blacksburg, Virginia, before killing himself.

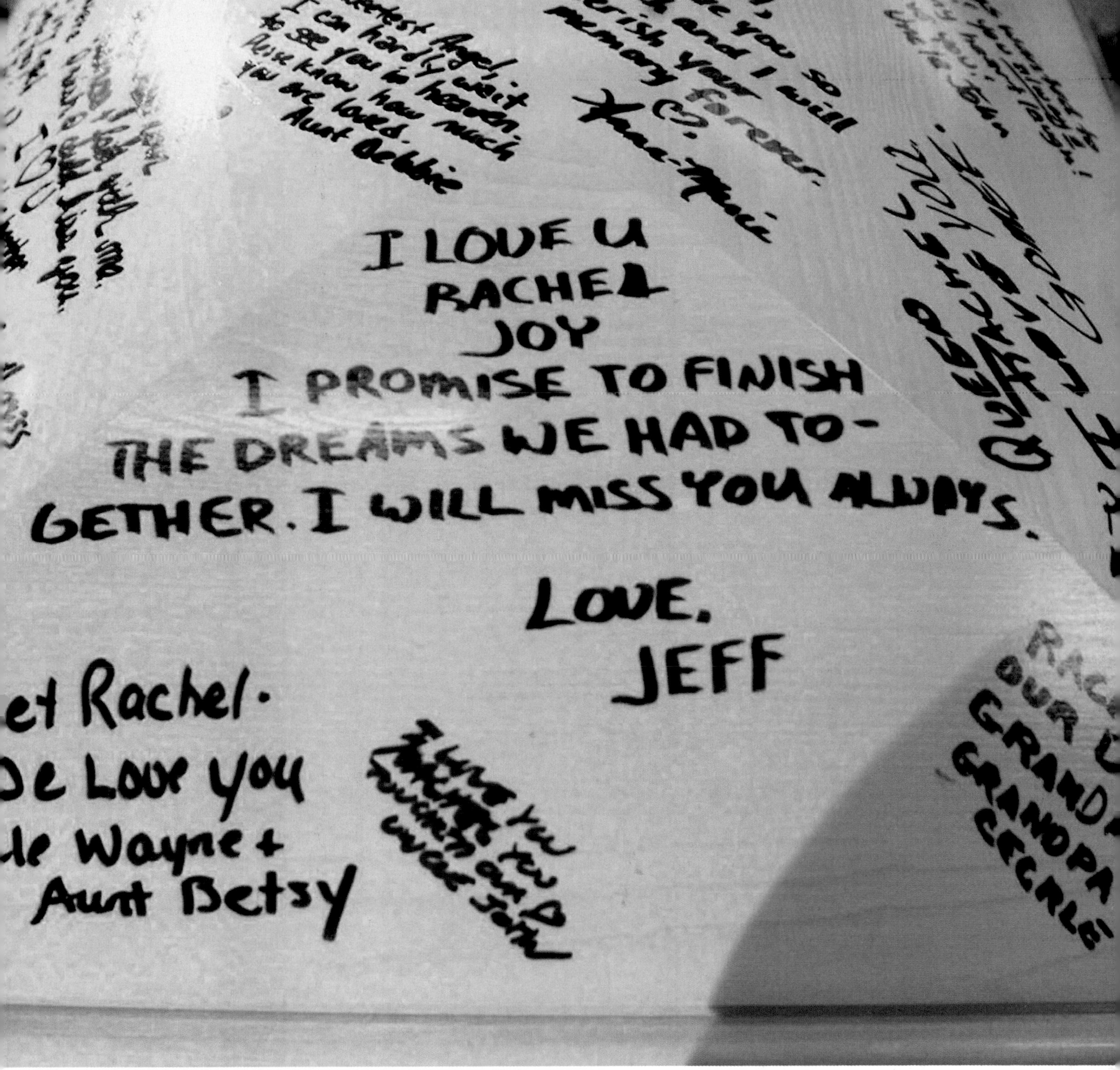

I LOVE U
RACHEL
JOY
I PROMISE TO FINISH
THE DREAMS WE HAD TO-
GETHER. I WILL MISS YOU ALWAYS.

LOVE,
JEFF

et Rachel.
De Love you
le Wayne +
Aunt Betsy

The casket bearing Columbine High School shooting victim Rachel Joy Scott is signed with notes of remembrance from family members. *AP Images*

Bush, Gore in cliffhanger

By Deborah Sharp
Excerpt from article published November 9, 2000

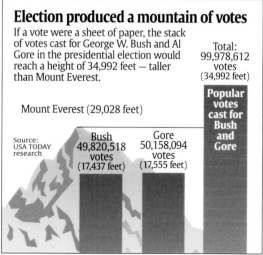

Published December 14, 2000

Election produced a mountain of votes

If a vote were a sheet of paper, the stack of votes cast for George W. Bush and Al Gore in the presidential election would reach a height of 34,992 feet — taller than Mount Everest.

Total:
99,978,612
votes
(34,992 feet)

Popular
votes
cast for
Bush
and
Gore

Mount Everest (29,028 feet)

Source:
USA TODAY
research

Bush
49,820,518
votes
(17,437 feet)

Gore
50,158,094
votes
(17,555 feet)

By April Umminger and Bob Laird, USA TODAY

MIAMI — The race for the U.S. presidency hinged Wednesday on a historic recount of Florida ballots that could give an electoral victory to Texas Gov. George W. Bush despite Vice President Al Gore's apparent win in the popular vote.

Republican and Democratic lawyers flew in to monitor the recount, which state officials expected to finish this evening. As the White House hung in the balance, Republicans retained a slim congressional majority despite Democratic gains in both the House and Senate.

If Bush holds his tiny lead in Florida, which is key to an Electoral College victory, it would be the first time since 1994 that the White House, the House and the Senate were controlled by one party. Republicans haven't been in that position since 1952.

However, the GOP's congressional majority is among the narrowest in history — initial vote totals suggest a five-seat margin in the House and perhaps a single seat in the Senate. Moreover, whoever wins the presidency is unlikely to capture 50% of the popular vote, making it tough to claim a strong mandate.

"There is immediately a problem of legitimacy," Rutgers University political scientist Ross Baker says. "The value of a single vote in a Congress this closely divided is magnified enormously. . . . These ambitious agendas laid out by Bush and Gore will not see the light of day, irrespective of who's chosen. The chances of a large tax cut are virtually nil."

A supporter of Democratic presidential candidate Al Gore displays a sticker calling for the continuation of hand recounting of presidential ballots on November 14, 2000, in West Palm Beach, Florida. *Roberto Schmidt/AFP/Getty Images*

Demonstrators rally in front of the U.S. Supreme Court prior to arguments by lawyers for Al Gore and George W. Bush. In a 5-4 decision, the Supreme Court ended the Florida recount, handing the presidency to Bush. *Tim Dillon/USA TODAY*

Bush showed a lead of about 1,700 votes in Florida, which holds the 25 electoral votes needed to give him the 270 required to win the White House. Should he win, it would be the third time in U.S. history and the first time since 1888 that a president has reached electoral victory while losing the popular vote.

Gore appeared to have captured the majority of ballots nationwide by fewer than 100,000 votes out of about 100 million cast.

"I'm confident," Bush said in a statement with running mate Dick Cheney. Calling the election "one of the most exciting races in American history," Bush vowed to bring the country together if he wins. "America has a long tradition of uniting once the election is over."

Gore, appearing with his running mate, Sen. Joe Lieberman, D-Conn., made no predictions about the race, but cautioned against a "rush to judgment." But he pledged to accept the electoral vote. "Our Constitution is the whole foundation of our freedom and it must be followed faithfully."

In addition to the Florida recount, which is required by state law because of the close tally, some Democratic activists and union leaders called for a probe of alleged problems in the state's vote....

Green Party candidate Ralph Nader won a significant minority of votes in Florida, Oregon and several other close states. Exit polls show that nearly half of his backers would have supported Gore in a two-way race with Bush, suggesting that Nader probably cost Gore a Florida win — and the White House.... ■

"We can unite"

By Kathy Kiely
Excerpt from article published December 14, 2000

The two rivals in the most protracted and rancorous presidential election in more than a century ended their contest Wednesday night with a common call for the nation to unite behind President-elect George W. Bush.

"I was not elected to serve one party, but to serve one nation. The president of the United States is the president of every single American, of every race and every background," Bush declared in a victory speech that he was forced to wait 36 days to deliver.

His Democratic foe, Al Gore, endorsed those sentiments in seven minutes of bittersweet remarks from his suite of vice-presidential offices, where he formally relinquished his claim on the White House next door. "What remains of partisan rancor must now be put aside," he said before ending his campaign on a note of wry humor.

Recalling a slogan used effectively in 1992, when he and Bill Clinton defeated Bush's father, Gore declared: "And now, my friends, in a phrase I once addressed to others, 'It's time for me to go.' "

In his 12-minute speech, Bush outlined several policy goals on which he believes the starkly split nation should "find common ground." Among them: improved public schools, stronger financial underpinnings for Social Security and Medicare, tax cuts and a strengthened military.

"Together, guided by a spirit of common sense, common courtesy and common goals, we can unite and inspire the American citizens," said Bush, the first son of a president to follow his father into the nation's highest office since John Quincy Adams in 1824.... ■

President Clinton and Hillary Rodham Clinton pose with President-elect George W. Bush and Laura Bush in front of the White House, January 20, 2001, the day of Bush's inauguration. *AP Images*

2001

9/11

Rubble burns at the remains of
the destroyed World Trade Center
towers, September 12, 2001.
Spencer Platt/Getty Images

U.S. under attack

By Richard Willing and Jim Drinkard
September 12, 2001

A shocked and shattered nation went on full wartime alert Tuesday after terrorist attacks in New York City and Washington left an unknown number of killed and wounded and shook the nation as perhaps nothing had since the Japanese attack on Pearl Harbor nearly 60 years ago.

"Freedom itself was attacked this morning by a faceless coward, and freedom itself will be defended," President Bush said early Tuesday afternoon, from a Louisiana air base to which he had been evacuated.

they had evidence linking Osama bin Laden, Saudi-born sponsor of Islamic terrorism, to the attacks. Earlier, claiming to speak for bin Laden, a spokesman for the Taliban, the Afghan revolutionary Islamic movement, denied his involvement.

Bush spoke after apparently hijacked commercial airliners loaded with passengers crashed into both twin towers of the World Trade Center in New York City and the Pentagon near Washington during rush hour Tuesday morning. By 10:30 a.m., less than two hours after the first jet slammed into the first tower, both towers had collapsed. The coordinated strikes came without warning.

At the World Trade Center, site of a previous terrorist attack in 1993, witnesses described a nearly incomprehensible scene.

"It was like the building had been hit by an asteroid," said Marty Singer, senior manager of a computer store one block from the 110-story towers.

"Fire was shooting out of the side. I saw at least 15 people jump out of the first building. Two were holding hands. I looked away. I couldn't take it anymore."

At about 10:40 a.m., a fourth hijacked jet crashed near Somerset County Airport near Johnstown, Pennsylvania. Federal officials surmise that it was en route to the Washington area to participate in the attack.

Smoke billows from the Pentagon on September 11, 2001. This photo was taken by Jym Wilson, a USA TODAY photo editor, looking out the window of the USA TODAY corporate office.
Jym Wilson/USA TODAY

Death and injury tolls were not immediately available, but were expected to reach into the thousands.

"Make no mistake — the United States will hunt down and punish those responsible for these cowardly acts," Bush said.

Three hours later, government sources said

Officials of American and United Airlines, which each owned two of the jets, reported that 266 people were aboard the four jets.

One, Barbara Olson, the wife of U.S. Solicitor General Theodore Olson, the federal government's

Wednesday, September 12, 2001

Special Edition
37 pages on America's day of terror

USA TODAY
NO. 1 IN THE USA

Carnage in New York
Horror, disbelief and thousands of victims. 6A

'Tears most of the day'
Coast to coast, Americans turn to each other. 8A

Pentagon in flames
As many as 800 believed dead at military HQ. 7A

'Act of war'
Terrorists strike; death toll 'horrendous'

**Bush to nation:
U.S. 'saw evil'**

Vows to avenge strikes. 16A

**Law enforcement
eyes bin Laden**

Warrants in Florida. 5A

**Crisis deepens
economic woes**

'The wrong time.' 1B

**86% say attacks
are acts of war**

USA TODAY/CNN Poll. 2A

**Crowds rush
blood centers**

'Touching' response. 10D

**Drama of day
in pictures**

Color pullout. 10-11A

top appeals lawyer, was on the airplane that crashed into the Pentagon. Barbara Olson, a former federal prosecutor and television commentator, apparently made a last-ditch effort to alert authorities to the plane's hijacking.

According to Theodore Olson, Barbara Olson and other passengers were herded into the back of the airplane by hijackers using "knife-like" instruments. She pulled out her cell phone and twice called her husband's office at the Justice Department. When she reached her husband, she told him the plane was being hijacked and urged him to quickly call the FBI.

The federal government moved quickly to place the nation on a full-scale security alert commensurate with an enemy attack.

Intelligence officials said that for at least the past 10 days they had anticipated a possible attack by followers of Osama bin Laden, the Saudi-born financier of Islamic terror groups. But the officials said they had expected the attacks, if any, to come against American targets abroad. American embassies and military installations overseas were on high alert Tuesday.

National security sources said they are working under the premise that the attacks will be renewed. No credible group has claimed responsibility for the attacks. But authorities believe that the coordination involved and the willingness of the attackers to die to kill others point to a radical Islamic group.

Bush cut short a trip to Florida to promote public education and flew to a military air base in Louisiana to protect his security. The CIA, sources said, advised him to deploy navy battle groups in the Atlantic to guard against renewed attacks. He convened a meeting of the National Security Council. Airports nationwide were closed, forcing the grounding of more than 3,600 aircraft, and the White House, U.S. Capitol, State and Justice departments and United Nations were evacuated.

Across the nation, the impact was immediate. In Glastonbury, Conn., a memorial service at St. Paul's Catholic Church attracted members of many faiths. In Oklahoma City, site of Timothy McVeigh's terrorist bombing in 1995, Donna Mackie volunteered to give blood and found 300 people had shown up ahead of her. In Sioux Falls, S.D., U.S. Marshal Lyle Swenson fought through near panic conditions to help close and evacuate the local airport.

"The way these things are timed, . . . you wonder what's coming next," he said.

Congressional leaders were moved to an unspecified secure location. America's intelligence community faced criticism for failing to ward off the attacks.

"(This is) a big intelligence failure," said Lawrence Eagleburger, secretary of state in 1992-93 under Bush's father.

"This is an act of war. This is the biggest equivalent to Pearl Harbor that we've had in 60 years."

Authorities believe one of the jets used in the World Trade Center attacks was an American Airlines 767 hijacked after leaving Boston. That jet struck a tower of the 110-floor World Trade Center at about 8:45 a.m. near the top, causing a large explosion and fire.

Less than 20 minutes later, at about 9:05 a.m., the World Trade Center's second tower was hit by another hijacked airliner in similar fashion. That tower partially collapsed from the force of the crash. The other tower fell later in the morning.

At 9:43, a third jet crashed into a western side of the Pentagon in the Washington suburb of Arlington, Va. That aircraft, also a commercial jet, was clearly visible to rush hour commuters as it swooped in low over Interstate 395, a feeder highway used by commuters from Virginia to Washington, D.C.

ABOVE: A sign leans on a utility pole near Shanksville, Pennsylvania, on November 6, 2001. United Flight 93 crashed in a field on an abandoned strip mine outside of Shanksville, killing 40 people. *Eileen Blass/USA TODAY*

OPPOSITE: New York City firefighters raise a flag at the site of the World Trade Center, September 11, 2001. Over 2,700 people, including over 300 firefighters, died at the site of the Twin Towers. *Ricky Flores/The Journal News*

ABOVE: Smoke rises over the Pentagon the morning of September 11. 184 people died at the Pentagon. *U.S. Navy/Getty Images*

RIGHT: Military personnel run from the burning Pentagon. *H. Darr Beiser/ USA TODAY*

In all, two 757s and two 767s were used, federal authorities and airlines officials said.

Eyewitnesses to both attacks described scenes that shocked the senses — jets headed calmly toward their targets, flying smoothly as if on final approach for a routine landing.

Then explosions, fireballs and chaos as bodies fell from the shattered buildings and survivors scattered on the ground outside.

"(The jet) was flying fast and low and the Pentagon was the obvious target," said Fred Gaskins, who was driving to his job as a national editor at USA TODAY near the Pentagon when the jet passed about 150 feet overhead. "It was flying very smoothly and calmly, without any hint that anything was wrong."

Aydan Kizildrgli, an English language student who is a native of Turkey, saw the jetliner bank slightly then strike a western wall of the huge five-sided building that is the headquarters of the nation's military.

"There was a big boom," he said. "Everybody was in shock. I turned around to the car behind me and yelled, 'Did you see that?' Nobody could believe it."

The scene inside the Pentagon was frantic. Tina Engberg, a civilian who works in the building's test and evaluation office, was watching television reports of the New York City attack when she felt a "ka-boom that shook the whole building.

"People started running and saying 'Get out of the building.' "

The Pentagon reported that about 100 people were killed or injured.

In New York City, the surreal sight of an airliner aimed for the World Trade Center made it difficult to comprehend that an attack was underway.

"A plane flew incredibly low over my apartment; we've never seen a plane this low before," said Nic Fulton, at home in his lower Manhattan apartment just north of the World Trade Center site.

To Deirdre Carson, working in Brooklyn, across the East River from the crash site, the crash sounded like a huge car wreck.

"I met a woman whose husband works on the 99th floor (of a World Trade Center tower) and she was just devastated," said Carson, who was working as an election monitor for Tuesday's New York City mayoral primary election. "She can't cross the bridge to get there and all the cell phones are out because the antennas are on top of the trade center.

"This is scary; this is big. The other (terrorist bombing of the World Trade Center, in 1993) was almost invisible," Carson said. "I'm not leaving Brooklyn today. Who knows what's next?"

Tara Colton, in an office building six blocks from the burning towers, said the sound of the blast was "like the world closing in on itself."

"When we opened the door to try to leave, the streets looked like a ghost town," she said.

"Everything (was) covered in ash and smoke."

New York City mayor Rudy Giuliani's strong reaction to 9/11 earned him the title "America's mayor." *Tim Dillon/USA TODAY*

An elevator worker from Irvington, N.J., was part of a crew working at the trade center's basement level loading dock.

"I heard a rumble and saw dust. I knew I had to get out," said the 50-year-old man, who would give his name only as "Wilbert."

He was encountered on a nearby street, caked with soot and searching for his 70-plus co-workers.

"I have to see if God blessed them as well as he blessed me," he said.

Greenwich Village resident Mark Flavin found himself trapped in a stalled subway train as he made his way to work at a law firm near the World Trade Center.

Flavin, with several other commuters, left the car and crawled to a nearby station and made his way to the street.

He emerged just before 10 a.m.

"I got hit with a tremendous blast (that) knocked me down the stairs," he said. "It was like we were in the middle of a tornado."

"I'm surprised I'm still alive."

Terrorism experts said that the date of the attack — Sept. 11 — holds no special significance in the Muslim religion or in the annals of Arab terror groups.

But they did note that an associate of Osama bin Laden was scheduled to be sentenced today (Sept. 12) for his role in the 1998 bombing of the American embassy in Tanzania that killed 213. The federal courthouse in New York City is located near the World Trade Center site in lower Manhattan.

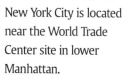

Investigators also declined to say how they believe the attacks were carried out. One working theory: The terrorists were trained pilots who over-whelmed cabin crews then flew the jets them-selves.

The ultimate impact on American life remains to be assessed. But Tony Cordesman, a military and Middle East expert at the Center for Strategic and International Studies in Washington, said it is likely to be profound.

"In one horrible moment, the need for homeland defense has gone from being a theoret-ical risk to a grim reality," he said. "No one of us — in government or coun-terterrorist experts outside government — believed that anyone was capable of launching an attack with this degree of lethality and coordination."

Sen. Chuck Hagel, R-Neb., said that "this changes everything."

"We essentially have been attacked at home. . . . We are changed forever-more." ◼

ABOVE: A woman looks at flyers that seek informa-tion on loved ones after the World Trade Center attacks. *Thomas Nilsson/Getty Images*

OPPOSITE: President Bush speaks with rescue work-ers, including firefighter Bob Beckwith (to his left), on September 14, 2001, with the rubble of the Twin Towers in the background. *Paul J. Richards/AFP/Getty Images*

Two beams of light shine from lower Manhattan in remembrance of the World Trade Center on the fourth anniversary of the September 11, 2001, terrorist attacks. *Todd Plitt/USA TODAY*

THE WAR IN IRAQ **2003–present**

U.S. Army Specialist Mitchell Roe, 20, of Canton, Michigan, watches Iraqi artillery positions, destroyed by close air support, burn on the horizon on April 2, 2003. *Jack Gruber/ USA TODAY*

From aboard the aircraft carrier USS Abraham Lincoln, President George W. Bush declares that "major combat operations in Iraq have ended," May 1, 2003.
Stephen Jaffe/AFP/Getty Images

May 2, 2003

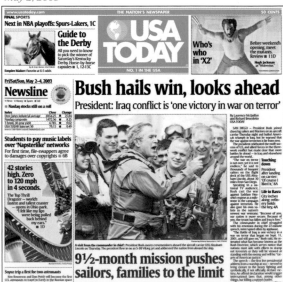

Last refuge a hole in ground

By Andrea Stone
Excerpt from article published December 15, 2003

In the end, the man who built 55 palaces was found in a hole in the ground. After eight months on the run, a dirty, disoriented Saddam Hussein was pulled from his hiding place just across the Tigris River from one of those palaces in Tikrit.

The root cellar-like hole was barely half the length of the huge, 13-foot-tall bronze Saddam busts removed recently from atop the dictator's luxurious Baghdad palace.

"It is rather ironic that he was in a hole in the ground across the river from these great palaces he built," said 4th Infantry Division commander Maj. Gen. Ray Odierno in Tikrit. . . .

"Anytime there were coalition forces nearby he just went down in that hole."

Styrofoam and a rug disguised the entrance to the hole, tucked inside a courtyard near a two-room mud hut where Saddam was apparently staying while above ground. Bricks and dirt at the opening completed the deception. A narrow vertical shaft led down six feet to a horizontal crawl space just big enough to lie down in.

Saddam, who was so phobic about germs that he used to require visitors to bathe before they met him, lay silently in his grave-like hole. A pipe and small fan connected to ground level provided ventilation.

When U.S. troops uncovered the square-cut vertical entrance to the hiding place, they saw a bedraggled man wordlessly staring up at them. They pulled him out into the evening air, lightly banging his head.

Saddam gave up without a fight. . . . ■

December 15, 2003

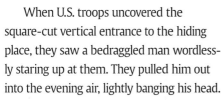
Two U.S. soldiers from the 1st Brigade of the 4th Infantry Division show the hole where toppled dictator Saddam Hussein was captured in Ad Dawr, near his hometown of Tikrit, December 15, 2003.
Mauricio Lima/AFP/Getty Images

"All-time high" in Baghdad violence

By Rick Jervis
Excerpt from article published October 12, 2006

An Iraqi weeps after a car bomb explosion in central Baghdad, February 12, 2007. The bomb ripped through a popular Shiite market and killed at least 40 people.
Ahmad Al-Rubaye/AFP/Getty Images

BAGHDAD — The number of sectarian killings each month in Baghdad has more than tripled since February, and the violence has not slowed despite a major offensive in the capital.

Death squads killed 1,450 people in September, up from 450 in February, according to U.S. military statistics. In the first 10 days of October, death squads have killed about 770 Iraqis.

The increase in death squad killings reflects the level of religious warfare that is now the largest threat to security in Iraq.

Lt. Col. Christopher Garver, a military spokesman, acknowledged violence in Baghdad is at an "all-time high" and said U.S. commanders, in coordination with their Iraqi counterparts, are continuing to adjust the security plan to try to reduce the violence. "We've been working to keep it peaceful, and we've been frustrated that the extremists keep perpetuating the number of attacks," Garver said.

U.S. forces are also caught in the violence. At least 37 American troops have been killed in combat this month, about half of them in or around Baghdad, where Iraqi and U.S. forces are attempting to loosen the grip of armed militias. The weekly average of U.S. deaths since President Bush declared the end of major combat operations in May 2003 has been about 14. . . . ■

At 4-year mark, a tug of war over direction of Iraq policy

By William M. Welch

Excerpt from article published March 20, 2007

The fourth anniversary of the start of the Iraq war was marked Monday by debate over a next step, with Democrats calling the current strategy a failure while Republicans said quitting now would create a nightmare.

"The American people have lost confidence in President Bush's plan for a war without end in Iraq," House Speaker Nancy Pelosi said. "That failed approach has been rejected by the voters . . . and it will be rejected by the Congress."

Senate Minority Leader Mitch McConnell, R-Ky., said America must be victorious in Iraq if the terrorists who struck on Sept. 11, 2001, are to be vanquished.

"Al-Qaeda's hope is to force a withdrawal of U.S. troops. That would be a victory for al-Qaeda and a nightmare for the Iraqis," McConnell said.

"For the sake of the Iraqi people, the stability of the region, and the security of America and our allies," he said, "we must not retreat from this fight; we must not succumb to the political expediency of the easy way out."

The anniversary comes as Congress mulls a $95.5 billion request from the Bush administration to maintain combat units in Afghanistan and Iraq and other areas. . . . ■

A soldier on the upper floor of the Saddam Hussein Presidential Palace waves the victory sign to other infantry who are securing the perimeter on April 7, 2003.
Jack Gruber/USA TODAY

OPPOSITE: Yusef (left) and Ahmed walk down the long barrel of an abandoned Iraqi tank while tending to cattle and sheep on October 16, 2003. *Jack Gruber/USA TODAY*

ABOVE: An Iraqi man carries his daughter by the wreckage of a car bomb explosion, March 20, 2007, in Baghdad. *Wathiq Khuzaie/ Getty Images*

LEFT: Children give a flower to one of the soldiers with Charlie Company/2-7 Infantry tasked with clearing any explosives or weapons left behind by retreating Iraqi soldiers in the Baghdad neighborhood of Firdos, April 14, 2003. *Jack Gruber/USA Today*

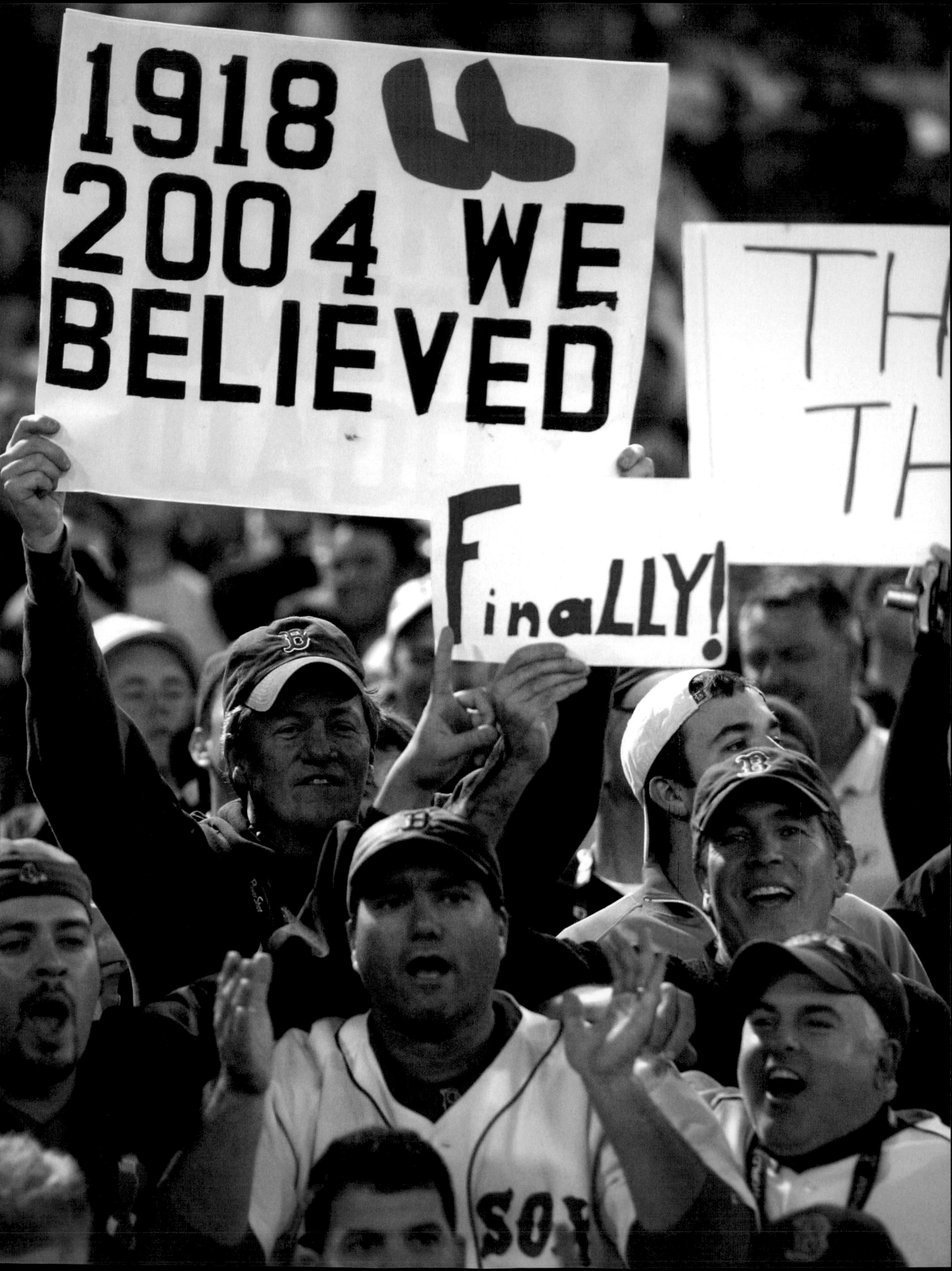
1918
2004 WE
BELIEVED
FinaLLY!

RED SOX REVERSE THE CURSE

2004

Curse RIP: 1918-2004

After decades of pain, Red Sox on top of world

By Mike Dodd
October 28, 2004

ST. LOUIS — The Boston Red Sox, the symbol of heartbreak and human foible to sports fans for nearly a century, are world champions.

No more curses. No more moral victories. No more next year.

The Red Sox completed an unprecedented 11-day turnaround Wednesday night when they defeated the St. Louis Cardinals 3-0 to win their first World Series since 1918.

The victory was as stunning as their inexplicable failures over the last 86 years — coming back from a three-games-to-none deficit against the New York Yankees in the American League Championship Series and sweeping the National League champion Cardinals, who won 105 games in the regular season.

"We did it, man. We're the champs," said Red Sox outfielder Manny Ramirez, who was voted Most Valuable Player of the Series.

Boston, the third consecutive wild-card team to claim baseball's championship, became the first team to win eight consecutive playoff games in a single postseason and never trailed even for an inning in winning four in a row against the Cardinals.

"We didn't want to let them back in it. We knew what happened to us," Red Sox manager Terry Francona said.

Nearly 5,000 Red Sox fans, who made most of the noise in Busch Stadium the last three innings, stood around the Boston dugout,

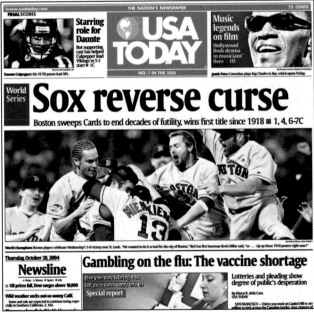

October 28, 2004

Red Sox fans celebrate after Boston defeated the St. Louis Cardinals in Game 4 of the World Series on October 27, 2004, at Busch Stadium in St. Louis, Missouri. Prior to 2004, the last time the Red Sox won the World Series was 1918. *Jed Jacobsohn/Getty Images*

cheering and chanting "Thank you, Red Sox" for more than 40 minutes after the game.

"No more having to go to Yankee Stadium and having to listen to '1918.' Finally," said Boston pitcher Derek Lowe, who threw seven shutout innings to record the biggest Red Sox victory in history.

St. Louis' collapse was just as shocking and complete as Boston's surge. The Cardinals managed just four hits Wednesday and a total of 13 in the final three games of the Series. Regulars Scott Rolen, Jim Edmonds and Reggie Sanders combined for one hit the entire series — Edmonds' bunt single against an over-shifted infield in his first at-bat in Game 1.

"They outplayed us in every category," Cardinals manager Tony La Russa said.

While many sports franchises have endured years of losing, no team has tantalized its faithful by coming so close and continually falling short.

The heartbreaks spawned the Curse of the Bambino, said to have started after Red Sox owner Harry Frazee sold Babe Ruth to the Yankees after the 1919 season. The legend soared in popularity after the Sox came within one strike of winning the 1986 Series, only to collapse as a ground ball went between first baseman Bill Buckner's legs.

This year, however, it's all heroes, many with their own tales of redemption.

Lowe, bounced from the starting rotation for the first round of the playoffs after faltering in September, allowed three hits in seven innings, retiring 13 Cardinals in a row after allowing a leadoff single in the first.

Ramirez, who was nearly traded in the aborted Alex Rodriguez deal, chipped in only a single Wednesday but hit .412 in the Series and .350 in the 14 games of the playoffs.

"God sent me back for a reason, and that's why I'm here," he said. "I proved a lot of people wrong."

Asked afterward how he wanted this team to be remembered, Francona had a simple answer.

"As winners," he said. ■

OPPOSITE: Slugger David Ortiz watches his first-inning three-run home run leave the park in the first game of the World Series. "Big Papi" had 139 RBIs during the 2004 regular season, and added another 19 in the playoffs. *Robert Deutsch/USA TODAY*

ABOVE: Blood seeps through Curt Schilling's sock in the first inning of Game 2. With a wall of stitches keeping his tendon in place, Schilling pitched six innings without allowing an earned run. The bloody sock was later given to the Hall of Fame. *H. Darr Beiser/ USA TODAY*

The Boston Red Sox celebrate their World Series win over the Cardinals, October 27, 2004. *Eileen Blass/USA TODAY*

Mary Bourgeois cries as she retrieves a statue of the Virgin Mary from the ruins of her home in Clermont Harbor, Mississippi, on September 4, 2005. She evacuated with her family before the storm hit.
H. Darr Beiser/USA TODAY

Eugene Green holds his baby, Eugene Green Jr., as they wait with other victims of Hurricane Katrina to be airlifted by helicopter from a highway overpass in New Orleans on September 4, 2005. *Mario Tama/Getty Images*

OLYMPICS ON
AMERICAN SOIL

Michael Johnson carries the U.S. flag after winning the
400 meter race at the 1996 Olympic Games in Atlanta,
Georgia. Johnson finished his Olympic career with five
gold medals: one in 1992, two in 1996, and two in 2000.
Jamie Squire/Getty Images

U.S. gold glows as flame dims

By Barbara Pearson
Excerpt from article published August 13, 1984

U.S. diver Greg Louganis competes during spring-board preliminaries of the 1984 Summer Olympics in Los Angeles. Louganis won two gold medals in 1984 and another two in 1988.
AP Images

LOS ANGELES — A glittering emotional closing ceremony brought the 1984 Summer Olympic Games to a rousing end Sunday, with 6,000 athletes from participating nations gathered in the Memorial Coliseum infield.

The USA dominated the medal chase with 174, including 83 gold, 61 silver and 30 bronze.

The USA team also broke the record of 80 gold medals set by the USA in 1904 and tied by the Russians in 1980. Next closest: Romania, 20 gold; West Germany, 59 total medals.

The 3-hour closing ceremony included a spectacular audience participation light show, a flashing "spaceship" landing and Lionel Richie singing "All Night Long" — accompanied by dozens of break-dancers and some athletes dancing and singing along.

USA stars at the Games:

▸ Carl Lewis, who matched Jesse Owens' 1936 record of four golds in track and field.

▸ Sprinter Valerie Brisco-Hooks, who tied Wilma Rudolph's three track golds.

▸ Five-time medalist gymnast Mary Lou Retton.

▸ Hurdler Edwin Moses, in his 90th straight victory.

▸ Joan Benoit, winning the first women's marathon.

Other Olympic highlights:

▸ An estimated 150 million Americans watched at least some of 180 hours broadcast by ABC-TV. . . . ■

ABOVE: Carl Lewis receives the baton from teammate Calvin Smith as he anchors the American team to victory in the 4x100 relay during the 1984 Summer Olympics. Lewis won four gold medals at the 1984 Olympics and finished his Olympic career with nine gold medals, the last in 1996. *Tony Duffy/ Getty Images*

LEFT: Mary Lou Retton on the balance beam during the 1984 Summer Olympics. She won the all-around gold with a dramatic perfect score on the vault, and captured four other medals. *Steve Powell/ Allsport/Getty Images*

Farewell to Atlanta

By Erik Brady

Excerpt from article published August 5, 1996

ATLANTA — Every Olympics has its signature moments. Over time, they become a kind of shorthand.

In 20 years, what will we remember of the Atlanta Games?

The bomb. And Kerri Strug.

We'll remember a lot more. But those two will pop up first, like a game of word association.

Try it yourself. Mexico City in 1968? Bob Beamon's leap and the black power salute. Munich in 1972? Eleven Israelis murdered and Mark Spitz's seven golds. Los Angeles in 1984? The boycott and Mary Lou.

And Carl.

The L.A. Games gave us Carl Lewis' Jesse Owens impersonation. And a dozen years later, here he is still providing the definition for defining moments. . . .

Lewis made time stand still. Michael Johnson blew right past it.

Sprinters defeat time in fractions of seconds. So it was for Johnson at the 400 meters. He broke the Olympic record by a hundredth of a second, leaving all other runners in his wake.

Then came the 200, and more magic. Johnson's golden shoes blazed around the track, blowing past the world's best while breaking his own world record by 0.34 seconds. In a sprinter's world, that is not just breaking a record, that is demolishing it. It felt so good, Johnson even smiled.

The Olympics can coax smiles or tears from any of us, as when Muhammad Ali lit the Olympic flame at the opening ceremonies. He won boxing gold at Rome in 1960. Now he stood on the world stage once more, a vision in white, shaking with Parkinson's syndrome, his presence burning brighter than the flame itself. . . . ■

OPPOSITE: U.S. gymnastics coach Bela Karolyi carries an injured Kerri Strug after she received her gold medal in the team competition at the 1996 games. Strug competed in the vault despite a sprained ankle. *Doug Pensinger/ Getty Images*

ABOVE: Gwen Torrance, Inger Miller, Gail Devers and Christy Gains celebrate after winning the gold medal in the 4x100 relay during the 1996 games. *Simon Bruty/ Getty Images*

Real life is golden for Hughes

By Vicki Michaelis
Excerpt from article published February 23, 2002

SALT LAKE CITY — Through her first few hours as America's newest ice princess, Sarah Hughes discovered the lure of an Olympic gold medal.

Her sisters, brothers and parents wanted to hold it, turn it over, make sure it was real.

"I think sometimes people were more interested in the medal than me," she said Friday morning, less than 14 hours after beating U.S. team-mate Michelle Kwan and Russian Irina Slutskaya to stun the skating world. . . .

"Her picture was on the front page of [her high school] school newspaper," her father said Friday, the day her picture was on the front page of newspapers across the country. "For a teenaged kid, that's a pretty big deal."

The gold medal is a big deal, too, but Hughes already is looking ahead to a test she's facing this spring.

"My next goal is to get in the high 1500s on my SATs," said Hughes, a high school junior. . . .

Thursday night, she couldn't believe her own fortune. She came into the Olympic women's figure skating final in fourth place. For the long program, she had to skate before the four competitors ahead of her in the standings.

"I really had nothing to lose. I thought there was no way in the world I could win," she said.

She completed her program, which included two triple-triple combination jumps as well as a triple-double, with almost carefree ease. Her smile grew wider as she skated, and when she was done, with the crowd on its feet and so loud she couldn't hear the end of her music, she said to all of them as much as herself, "Wow!"

"I thought, you know what, no matter what, that's my gold medal performance," she said. . . . ■

OPPOSITE: U.S. snowboarder Ross Powers gets some "big air" on the halfpipe during a qualification run in the 2002 Olympic games. Powers captured the gold medal in the event, the second medal of his Olympic career. *Jack Gruber/USA TODAY*

ABOVE: Sarah Hughes of the USA performs in the figure skating exhibition during the 2002 Salt Lake City Winter Olympic Games. Hughes won the gold and fellow American Michelle Kwan won the bronze. *Doug Pensinger/Getty Images*

OPPOSITE TOP LEFT: U.S. wrestler Kurt Angle reacts to his gold medal win in the 100 kg class of freestyle wrestling at the 1996 Atlanta Games. *AP Images*

OPPOSITE BOTTOM: David Robinson, Scottie Pippen, Mitch Richmond, Reggie Miller, Karl Malone, and Shaquille O'Neal were part of the team that defeated Yugoslavia 95–69 for the gold in men's basketball in 1996. *AP Images*

OPPOSITE TOP RIGHT: U.S. gold medalists Jill Bakken and Vonetta Flowers in action in the women's bobsled during the 2002 Salt Lake City Winter Olympic Games. *Mike Powell/Getty Images*

BOTTOM LEFT: U.S. speedskater Apolo Anton Ohno captured the gold medal in the 1,500 meter and the silver medal in the 1,000 meter during the 2002 Olympics. *H. Darr Beiser/USA TODAY*

TOP RIGHT: U.S. marathoner Joan Benoit won the gold medal at the 1984 Summer Olympics in Los Angeles. *H. Darr Beiser/ USA TODAY*

BOTTOM RIGHT: Andre Agassi competes during the first round of men's Olympics tennis in 1996. Agassi, who retired in 2006 with eight career grand slam wins, won the gold in 1996. *Olivier Morin/AFP/Getty Images*

1986, 2003 **TRAGEDIES IN SPACE**

The space shuttle Challenger blasts
off from the Kennedy Space Center
in Florida on January 28, 1986.
MPI/Getty Images

"Future belongs to brave"

Reagan backs space program

By David Colton
Excerpt from article published January 29, 1986

The fiery image lingers — and the search for answers begins today to the USA's worst space disaster.

In a horrible flash seen repeatedly by millions on TV, a crew of seven, including teacher Christa McAuliffe, died instantly Tuesday when the shuttle Challenger exploded just one minute and 12 seconds after liftoff.

Flames appeared along the left booster rocket 72 seconds into the flight — NASA said it stopped getting data from the shuttle 74 seconds after liftoff.

"A day we wish we could have pushed back forever," said former astronaut Sen. John Glenn, D-Ohio.

"We mourn seven heroes," President Reagan — who initiated the teacher in space project — told the nation in a speech Tuesday.

But reaffirming his backing of the space program, Reagan said: "The future doesn't belong to the faint-hearted, it belongs to the brave."

"Oh my God, no," said Nancy Reagan when she saw the explosion live in the White House at 11:39 a.m. EST.

The impact ranged from the White House to USA classrooms: All eyes were on a fruitless search in the Atlantic, where only pieces of debris were found.

▸ Reagan cancelled his State of the Union address after watching endless replays of the $1.2 billion Challenger exploding in a rolling ball of flames.

▸ The USA's space shuttle program was put on indefinite hold until a NASA investigating team can determine a cause.

"We will not speculate as to the specific cause of the explosion based on footage" of the accident, said Jess Moore, NASA's shuttle chief.

▸ At McAuliffe's high school in Concord, N.H., 200 students cheered and blew party horns at liftoff. Then came gasps, disbelief and silence.

"I kept hoping maybe they're joking," said Concord student Carrie Harrison, 17.

Debris from the Challenger rained down for 45 minutes after nearly 500,000 gallons of fuel exploded 10 miles high. The glare was instantly visible to thousands of onlookers, including McAuliffe's parents on the ground.

The last transmission from Challenger: "Roger. Go to throttle up."

Early reports found "no abnormalities" apparent to flight controllers before the blast. . . . ∎

Christa McAuliffe, a New Hampshire schoolteacher, was a crewmember on Challenger. *USA TODAY*

ABOVE: The space shuttle Challenger explodes shortly after lifting off from Kennedy Space Center. The explosion was blamed on faulty O-rings in the shuttle's booster rockets. The Challenger's crew was honored with burials at Arlington National Cemetery. *AP Images*

LEFT: President Ronald Reagan addresses the nation from the White House after the Challenger explosion. "We will never forget them nor the last time we saw them this morning, as they prepared for their journey and waved goodbye and slipped the surly bonds of Earth to touch the face of God," Reagan said in one of his most famous speeches. *Diana Walker/Time Life Pictures/Getty Images*

Some remains found in unprecedented search

By Dan Reed, Martin Kasind and Larry Copeland
Excerpt from article published February 3, 2003

NACOGDOCHES, Texas — Police, firefighters and volunteers walked shoulder to shoulder through fields and woods in eastern Texas on Sunday as they searched for remains of the seven crewmembers of the shuttle Columbia and for debris scattered across hundreds of square miles of piney forests and small towns.

NASA announced that remains of some of the crewmembers had been found.

The day after Columbia fell to Earth in a shower of smoking and spinning metal, a widespread search moved into high gear. The recovery workers used everything from horses and four-wheel drive vehicles to Air Force F-16 fighters and satellite gear.

In addition to the search for bodies, authorities hoped to find key parts of the shuttle to speed the investigation of what went wrong.

President Bush declared a national emergency in eastern Texas and ordered the Federal Emergency Management Agency to coordinate search efforts. NASA was directing an investigation from a command center at Barksdale Air Force Base at Bossier City, La., where the collected debris will be trucked. Later it will be assembled into a rough outline of the wreck.

The hunt for clues to the tragedy swept up hundreds of ordinary citizens and federal, state and local emergency workers and investigators.

By late Sunday, chunks of debris had been found in 33 Texas counties. Officials were fielding 150 calls an hour reporting sightings in Nacogdoches County alone.

But key parts of the wreckage might not be found for weeks, said Sue Kennedy, Nacogdoches County's emergency management coordinator. "It may be months from now when some hunter out on his land comes across some debris," she said.

Kennedy said NASA had put out a special call for "any piece that might be part of the control section" of the shuttle. Parts of the cockpit were among items found, officials said.

The first human remains linked to the shuttle were found just before nightfall Saturday. A charred torso, thighbone and skull were discovered on a rural road in Hemphill, east of Nacogdoches.

"I wouldn't want anybody seeing what I saw," said Mike Gibbs, a hospital employee who found the remains. By Sunday morning, Roger Cody, who lives nearby, had built a cross to mark the spot where the remains were found.

Some of the debris that fell was charred or scorched. Other parts appeared to have been twisted by heat or impact. . . . ■

ABOVE: A portrait of the Columbia crew is displayed on February 2, 2003, in front of a memorial dedicated to all of the astronauts who have died since the beginning of America's manned spaceflight program.
Tim Dillon/USA TODAY

OPPOSITE: Leisa Pate and her daughters stand near a piece of the Columbia shuttle, February 2, 2003. The debris fell in the yard of Pate's brother, who honored it by placing a flag flying at half staff nearby.
H. Darr Beiser/USA TODAY

 Stephen G. Breyer, 1994

 Clarence Thomas, 1991

 John Paul Stevens, 1975

 Anthony M. Kennedy, 1988

ABOVE: The current lineup of United States Supreme
Court Justices, and the year they each joined the court.
Tim Dillon/USA TODAY

Ruth Bader Ginsburg, 1993

Samuel A. Alito, Jr., 2006

Antonin Scalia, 1986

David H. Souter, 1990

John Roberts, 2005

Other U.S. Supreme Court Justices of the past 25 years

William J. Brennan, Jr., 1956-1990
Byron Raymond White, 1962-1993
Thurgood Marshall, 1967-1991
Harry A. Blackmun, 1970-1994

Lewis F. Powell, Jr., 1972-1987
William H. Rehnquist, 1972-2005
Sandra Day O'Connor, 1981-2006

PART TWO
GLOBAL HEADLINES

1989

SLAUGHTER IN
TIANANMEN SQUARE

Students gather April 22, 1989, to mourn the death of Hu Yaobang, a reformist official who had been ousted as Communist Party chief two years earlier. Hu's death was the catalyst for the events that unfolded in Tiananmen Square, as the large crowds expanded and protestors aired a range of grievances against the government. At times over a million people packed into Tiananmen Square.
Catherine Henriette/AFP/Getty Images

China: "Slaughter" in the streets

By Johanna Neuman
Excerpt from article published June 5, 1989

ABOVE: A "Statue of Liberty" was erected in Tiananmen Square on May 30, 1989. About 200,000 people were in the square when the statue was unveiled. A portrait of Mao Tse-tung is visible in the distance.
Toshio Sakai/AFP/Getty Images

OPPOSITE: A protester in Tiananmen Square holds up a sign that reads "We no longer trust dirty public servants. We trust Mr. Democracy."
Forrest Anderson/Time Life Pictures/Getty Images

Chinese troops opened fire again early today on some of the hundreds of thousands of pro-democracy protesters near Beijing's Tiananmen Square.

The outbreak — where about 50 soldiers fired at a crowd of 3,000 on a main Beijing street — followed bloody weekend confrontations that left at least 500 dead.

Trouble in Beijing began just after midnight Saturday (11 a.m. EDT) when soldiers — in tanks, on foot, in armored personnel carriers — drove into crowds, firing guns.

Thousands may be dead from the fighting, which left the Beijing sky lit by flames, its streets littered with the injured and dead. The 33-foot replica of the Statue of Liberty erected by students was burned.

The violence was roundly condemned throughout the world, and Congress is pressuring President Bush to act.

As the U.S. weighed options:

‣ Protesters blocked streets in Shanghai, China's largest city, where workers called for a general strike.

‣ Tearful Chinese students marched in Taipei; Paris; London; San Francisco; New York; Washington; Los Angeles; Oslo, Norway; Vancouver, Canada.

‣ In Hong Kong, which reverts to Chinese rule in 1997, 200,000 rallied in mourning.

‣ About 1,000 students in Wuhan reportedly cut railway traffic between Guang Zhou and Beijing, lying on tracks to prevent military transports.

In Washington, Rep. Stephen Solarz, D-N.Y., warned if Bush doesn't act, "Congress will."

"It would be politically unacceptable and morally unthinkable to continue to sell arms to a country engaged in the wanton slaughter of its people."

Sen. Jesse Helms, R-N.C., demanded "all military cooperation and sharing of technology be terminated immediately."

Bush meets today with congressional leaders.

Chinese leader Deng Xiaoping, hospitalized with prostate cancer, gave the order to shoot from bed: "Even if they're functioning out of ignorance they are still participating and must be suppressed. In China, even 1 million people can be considered a small sum." . . . ■

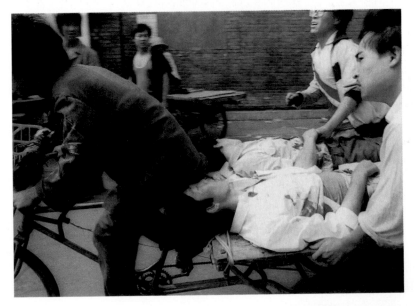

OPPOSITE: A man blocks a line of tanks in Tiananmen Square on June 5, 1989. When the tanks veered left, he moved left. When the tanks moved forward, he held his ground. Bystanders eventually pulled him away, ending a five-minute stand-off captured by TV cameras. His identity is still unknown. *AP Images*

ABOVE: Pro-democracy demonstrators celebrate as they stop a military truck filled with soldiers on its way to Tiananmen Square on May 20, 1989. *Catherine Henriette/AFP/Getty Images*

LEFT: A rickshaw driver ped-dles wounded people to a nearby hospital on June 4, 1989. *AP Images*

"The Wall is gone"

Berliners celebrate at "relic of the past"

By Juan J. Walte

Excerpt from article published November 10, 1989

AT THE BERLIN WALL — East Germans — told they were free to travel anywhere — wept, hugged, pranced and kissed in both halves of divided Berlin today after East Germany opened its borders for the first time since 1961.

The joyous scene occurred at the world's monument to communism, symbol for 28 years of the Cold War and testament to 191 East Germans who've perished trying to crawl, climb or even fly over it.

Berliners celebrated through the night, climbing atop the concrete barrier and chipping away at its surface with hammers. Others danced in delight at Checkpoint Charlie and the Brandenburg Gate.

Strangers embraced strangers as cars packed with East Germans and others paraded through West Berlin.

Highlights of a dizzying day that capped a

A man hammers away at the Berlin Wall, November 12, 1989, as the border between East and West Germany falls after 28 years. The two Germanies officially reunited October 3, 1990. *AP Images*

ABOVE: A couple blow a kiss to each other through a crack in the Berlin Wall.
Andreas Pollok/Getty Images

OPPOSITE: An East German border guard offers a flower through a gap in the Berlin Wall on the morning of November 10, 1989. The fall of the Berlin Wall was the most visible in a series of repudiations of communism throughout Eastern Europe and the Soviet Union.
Tom Stoddart/Getty Images

two-month pro-democracy campaign:

▸ East Germany's new leader, Egon Krenz, promised free elections and new laws on freedom of assembly, association and the press.

▸ "This is a historic day," said West Berlin Mayor Walter Momper. "We will welcome the people with open arms."

▸ Up to 4,000 East Germans an hour were reported entering Czechoslovakia at one crossing, 10 times the number a few hours earlier.

▸ President Bush called it a "dynamic development . . . clearly a big development in terms of human rights."

▸ Senate Majority Leader George Mitchell urged East Germany to "take the final step and tear that Wall down."

▸ West German Chancellor Helmut Kohl called for face-to-face talks with East German leader Krenz to discuss East Germany's political crisis.

▸ Fifteen prominent communists in East Berlin wrote to the Central Committee suggesting the Wall be torn down.

"It is also imaginable . . . that the Wall will become a relic of the past."

An estimated 1.2 million to 1.4 million East Germans will resettle in the West. . . . ■

Moscow students take a break on a toppled statue of Stalin in a park in Moscow, Russia, on September 11, 1991. As communism fell, the Soviet Union dissolved into its member states, the largest of which is Russia. The Soviet flag last flew over the Kremlin on December 25, 1991. *AP Images*

NELSON MANDELA'S
71-YEAR STRUGGLE FOR FREEDOM

Timeline originally published February 12, 1990
Photo: *Hamish Blair/Liaison/Getty Images*

1918	**1944**	**1948**	**1952**	**1956**	**1960**
Born; father is tribal chief.	Joins African National Congress, dedicated to non-violent protest of anti-black laws.	Nationalist (whites-only) Party elected and legalizes apartheid policy of racial separation; Mandela leads campaign of civil disobedience.	Leads campaign of anti-apartheid protests (8,000 people arrested, 14 killed).	Acquitted on charges of advocating revolution.	After 69 killed in Sharpeville massacre, Mandela jailed briefly under government state of emergency.

1961
Becomes head of Spear of the Nation, underground paramilitary branch of the ANC, and leads campaign of sabotage against targets symbolizing apartheid.

1962
Arrested for inciting riot, leaving country; sentenced to five years in prison.

1964
After ANC headquarters raided, Mandela taken from prison, put on trial for sabotage and treason; sentenced to life.

1984
Rejects offer to leave prison, settle in black tribal "homeland" of Transkei.

1985
Rejects offer of release if he renounces violence.

1990
Released from prison.

FAREWELL TO DIANA

The coffin of Diana, Princess of
Wales, is carried through the streets
of London on September 6, 1997.
The royal flag covers the coffin.
Tim Graham/Getty Images

Villagers in Krueng Raya, Indonesia, salvage building materials to carry into the hills and use to construct shelters in refugee camps away from the ocean, January 15, 2005. *Jack Gruber/USA TODAY*

Members of a search and rescue team pray over the body of a young girl in Banda Aceh, Indonesia, January 20, 2005. The search and rescue team members buried the child in a remote location, noted the grave site and took a necklace she was wearing in the hopes of identifying the child at a later date with family members. *Jack Gruber/USA TODAY*

THE PASSING OF POPE JOHN PAUL II

2005

Thousands drawn to St. Peter's to mourn

By Marco R. Della Cava
April 4, 2005

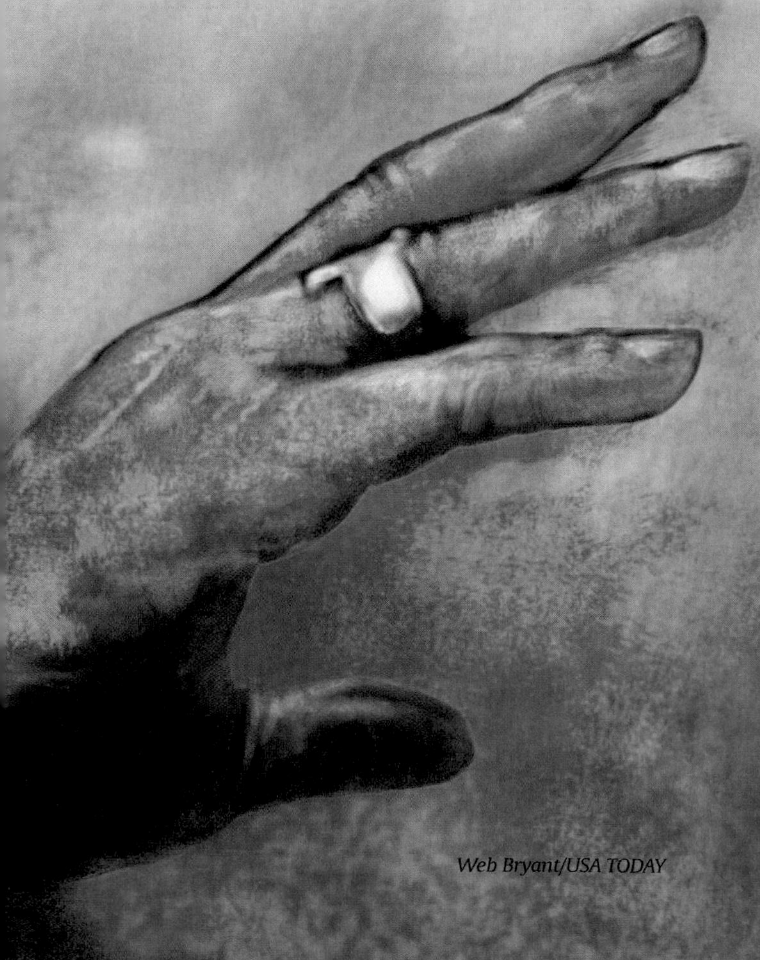

ROME — Even by the standards of the Eternal City, a faith-steeped haven dotted with churches, Sunday's Mass for Pope John Paul II had remarkable resonance.

Tens of thousands of people filled St. Peter's Square to both mourn the passing and celebrate the life of John Paul, who became a world spiritual and moral leader with influence far beyond the Roman Catholic Church.

From families dressed in their finest clothes to tourists with cameras around their necks, worshipers alternately dabbed at tears and erupted in applause during a sun-dappled morning Mass that featured a reading of the pontiff's final religious message.

"I came here to be part of an important moment," said Anja Tegeler, 29, a German-language teacher from Lubbecke now living in Rome. The pope "was in so much pain for so long, it is a relief for it to be over for him."

The pope's passing nearly a dozen hours earlier had given many the time to transform their emotions from grief to appreciation for his 26-year papacy.

"We felt we had to be with him today. After all, he's the only pope my generation has ever known,"

Web Bryant/USA TODAY

ABOVE: Mourners fill St. Peter's Square at the Vatican before the start of the funeral for Pope John Paul II on April 8, 2005. *Eileen Blass/USA TODAY*

OPPOSITE: Joanne Nolan places flowers next to a statue of Pope John Paul II at The Cathedral Basilica of St. Louis in St. Louis, Missouri, on April 3, 2005. *Robert Deutsch/USA TODAY*

said Cristina Nozza of Rome, pushing her sleeping 10-month-old. She and husband Gianluca, a bus driver, made their way here as soon as his morning shift ended.

Above the cobblestone square where many had camped for the night, the windows of the papal apartment were dark and shuttered, a change from the illumination that had drawn prayerful crowds as John Paul's life ebbed away. The pope's quarters were sealed after his death, in keeping with church tradition.

Mourners from all stages of life came to pay their respects.

Crying babies were hushed by parents. Italian Boy Scouts and Brownies struggled on tiptoe to catch a glimpse of the Italian dignitaries lining the steps of St. Peter's.

In the oval-shaped piazza, filled with as many as 100,000 people, the atmosphere was heavy with respect. Police officers, seeing little need for crowd control, found themselves making the sign of the cross at appropriate moments.

There was spontaneous applause when the giant television screens showed images of John Paul as well as the pope's last religious exhortation, written just before Easter, which focused on "God's gift of redemption" to a world "dominated by the power of evil, selfishness and fear."

While homemade flags of many nations fluttered in the breeze, the white and red colors of John Paul's native Poland dominated.

"I do feel a connection with the pope, but I don't think it's because he's Polish. He connected with the whole world," said Anna Zieba, 24, of Kielche, Poland, who has spent five years in Rome.

Referring to the pope's birth name, Karol Wojtyla, she said, "We need another Wojtyla, now more than ever." ■

PART THREE
TRENDS AND CHANGES

THE AIDS PANDEMIC

Several hundred people gather for a candlelight vigil to remember those who have died of AIDS on World AIDS Day, December 1, 2006, in Washington, D.C. World AIDS Day was created by the World Health Organization in 1988 to raise awareness of the AIDS pandemic. *Chip Somodevilla/Getty Images*

Justine Namuli's coffin is carried from her village home to her family's cemetery in Nsanvu, Uganda, on February 6, 1999. Namuli died of AIDS at the age of 27. *Jym Wilson/USA TODAY*

In Africa, unimagined levels of HIV

By Steven Sternberg
July 8, 2002

BARCELONA — AIDS is slashing the life expectancy of people in the hardest-hit countries in sub-Saharan Africa to levels not seen since the late 1800s, according to a study released Sunday by the U.S. Census Bureau.

In Botswana, a person who once might have expected to live to age 72 now will be lucky to reach 40. Already, more people in Botswana are dying than being born, a negative growth rate that by 2010 will spread to South Africa, Lesotho, Malawi and Zimbabwe.

"Even 10 years ago, we did not expect to see this," the report's author, Karen Stanecki, said at the 14th International AIDS Conference that began here Sunday. "We never expected to see HIV prevalence levels this high."

Without massive treatment programs, the hardest-hit countries will see their most productive people die off, leaving only older people and orphans who will have to scrabble to survive without social supports or education.

Last year, 1 million children lost teachers to AIDS, says Peter Piot, director of the Joint United Nations Programme on HIV/AIDS (UNAIDS). "AIDS is already starting to destabilize nations in Africa," he says.

By 2020, men between the ages of 15 and 44 will outnumber women in these age groups, prompting men to migrate in search of mates or choose partners among much younger women — potentially exposing even more young women to HIV. "These are population structures we've never seen before," Stanecki said.

About 70% of the 37 million people with AIDS worldwide live in sub-Saharan Africa, which contains only 11% of the global population. Already, almost one of every 10 people in the region is HIV positive, compared with less than 1% of adults in the USA. Since the beginning of the epidemic, more than 15 million Africans have died from AIDS, 2.2 million of them last year alone.

Uganda and Senegal still represent two of the best examples of the power of prevention worldwide. In Kampala, HIV prevalence dropped from a peak of 30% in 1993 to 11% in 2000. In Senegal, aggressive programs have prevented AIDS from gaining a toehold.

Many AIDS-ravaged countries won't recover from the demographic devastation of the epidemic for decades, if at all. "It's going to take countries like South Africa half a century to recover from the effects of this," Stanecki said.

These trends are beginning to emerge in Thailand, Cambodia and Burma, though the impact is not yet as great. China and the former Soviet states have yet to feel the full brunt of AIDS because their epidemics are just gaining a toehold, she said.

China, fearful of the impact of AIDS, has launched a major prevention program, Piot said. But he noted that the response has not been as aggressive in many of the provinces, particularly the poorer ones. "There's still a lot of denial," he said. ∎

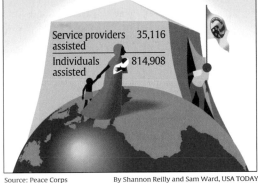

Published May 6, 2005

Volunteers fighting AIDS globally
About 3,100 Peace Corps volunteers — 40% of total volunteers — conducted HIV/AIDS activities around the world in 2004, and nearly two-thirds of them served in Africa. The impact of volunteers' efforts:

Service providers assisted	35,116
Individuals assisted	814,908

Source: Peace Corps   By Shannon Reilly and Sam Ward, USA TODAY

WOMEN RISE
IN THE WORKPLACE

Wives gain, but still lag in salaries

By Calvin Lawrence Jr.
Excerpt from article published July 26, 1989

Working wives earned 23.3 percent more in 1987 than in 1981 while their husbands gained only 11.8 percent, a Census Bureau study shows.

But that increase failed to make much of a dent: Wives who worked full time in 1987 still earned only 57.3 percent of their husbands' average full-time salary.

That gap is an improvement over 1981's 54.9 percent, but "this shows that women are still segregated in ... women's jobs, and they're paid very poorly," says Deborah Meyer of 9 to 5, National Association of Working Women.

The bureau says pay for wives grew faster because:

▸ More worked full time — 50 percent, up from 44 percent.

▸ More were professionals and managers.

▸ Some husbands are now working only part time. Others have taken lower paying service jobs as manufacturing industries shrink.

Measured in 1987 dollars, the study shows wives:

▸ Averaged $13,245 in 1987, up from $10,744 in 1981 — including those working part time and seasonally. Working husbands earned $29,154 in 1987, vs. $26,075 in 1981.... ■

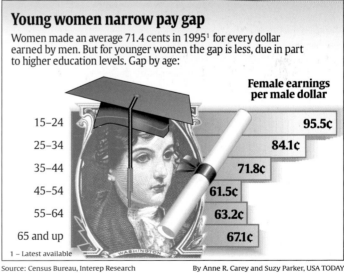

Published July 29, 1997

Young women narrow pay gap

Women made an average 71.4 cents in 1995[1] for every dollar earned by men. But for younger women the gap is less, due in part to higher education levels. Gap by age:

Female earnings per male dollar

Age	
15–24	95.5¢
25–34	84.1¢
35–44	71.8¢
45–54	61.5¢
55–64	63.2¢
65 and up	67.1¢

1 – Latest available

Source: Census Bureau, Interep Research

By Anne R. Carey and Suzy Parker, USA TODAY

OPPOSITE: Bridget Macaskill, CEO of OppenheimerFunds from 1995 to 2001.
Evan Kafka/Getty Images

Practically alone at the top

By Micheline Maynard
Excerpt from article published September 7, 1999

Geraldine Ferraro made history as the first woman on a major party's presidential ticket. Democrat Walter Mondale chose her to be his running mate in 1984.
Diana Walker/Time Life Pictures/Getty Images

DETROIT — Arriving early for a recent meeting with auto dealers, Christine Cortez was pouring herself a cup of coffee when one of the attendees asked her whether she felt out of place.

"Why?" Cortez asked. "Because you're the only woman in the room," the man said.

"If that bothered me, I would have gotten out of this industry 20 years ago," Cortez, DaimlerChrysler's vice president for fleet sales, told him.

These days, Cortez isn't alone, but she doesn't have much company. Among the American automakers, 14 women rank as corporate officers — from vice president to CEO — compared with 186 men.

That's better than in the early 1990s, when each company boasted just one or two female executives. And each of the Big Three automakers is aggressively driving to fill its pipeline with qualified female engineers, manufacturing experts, designers and marketing specialists who someday can sit in the driver's seat.

Says Saturn chief Cynthia Trudell: "As more women enter this environment, they will help influence it and change it. Someday, people like me will not be as unique."

But for now, she and her 13 counterparts remain oddities. Including auto suppliers and import automakers, 8% of industry executives are female, compared with 11.1% for all Fortune 500 companies. . . . ■

More women take CFO roles

By Matt Krantz
Excerpt from article published October 13, 2004

Hewlett-Packard CEO Carly Fiorina speaks before a group in Los Angeles on November 7, 2001. Fiorina headed Hewlett-Packard from 1999 to 2005.
David McNew/Getty Images

Women may be hitting the glass ceiling when it comes to getting into the CEO suite, but they're shattering it on the way into the CFO's office.

While a small percentage of the nation's biggest corporations have female CEOs, a rising and significant portion are promoting women into their top financial post: the chief financial officer.

Some 8.7% of companies in the Standard & Poor's 500, including house-hold names such as Yahoo, PepsiCo and Home Depot, now have female CFOs, according to a USA TODAY analysis of data from Hoover's, a service that collects information on companies. That's well above the 3.5% that have female chief operating officers and 1.8% with female CEOs.

While the number of female CEOs has hardly budged, in two years, the number of large companies with a female CFO has grown more than 20%, according to a study by Catalyst, which researches issues concerning women in business. . . . ◼

AMERICA'S ONLINE

Growth spurt causes traffic tie-ups on Internet

By Mike Snider
Excerpt from article published March 22, 1995

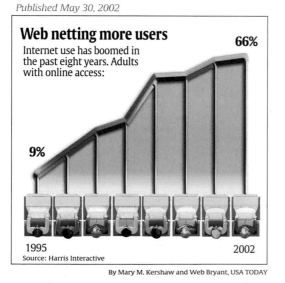

Published May 30, 2002

Web netting more users
Internet use has boomed in
the past eight years. Adults
with online access:

66%

9%

1995   2002

Source: Harris Interactive

By Mary M. Kershaw and Web Bryant, USA TODAY

Though more than 20 years old, the Internet is facing the biggest growth spurt of its life.

One burst of Net traffic two months ago on networks near Washington, D.C., caused an extremely rare occurrence: e-mail messages, transferred files and other data were lost. It was an example of both the unprecedented interest in the Internet and the strains the fascination is causing.

Internet access providers are signing up aspiring Net surfers as fast as they can. Meanwhile companies like Time Warner, Sony and Viacom, along with magazines like *Playboy* and *Penthouse*, are setting up shop on the World Wide Web, whose simplicity and stunning photos, sound and video are making it the hottest face of the Net. Heck, even Ragu spaghetti sauce has its own Web site.

"No communication system has ever grown this fast," says Internet Society president Vinton Cerf. He's often referred to as the "father of the Internet" for helping to develop the networking specifications that allow various kinds of computers to coexist on the Net. Cerf now designs networks for MCI.

The Internet was started by the Department of the Defense in the late

1960s as an attack-proof, widespread network of computer networks. It grew as a research-sharing vehicle with National Science Foundation involvement in the '80s.

Commercial, regional and other networks continue the expansion. Networks linked to the Net have grown from fewer than 5,000 in 1991 to more than 45,000 today; every 30 minutes another one connects.

The Internet's abilities have grown along with interest. Newsgroups, special-interest message-posting sites, have emerged as cyberspace meeting hubs — more than 12,000 at last count.

But e-mail and file transferring, the Net's primary objectives, also are booming. From the last two months of 1992 to today, e-mail messages have quadrupled from 230 million per month to about a billion.

Also, new software makes it easy to cruise the World Wide Web. But the extra work involved in transferring large visual and audio files adds a huge load to the Net.

Most longtime observers now accept that the Net is leaning "in the commercial direction," Cerf says. "Companies are beginning to realize that the Internet is the world's biggest focus group."

Originally a stand-alone online service,

America Online now offers its 2 million users Internet (though not yet Web) access.

In mid-January, Prodigy introduced its Web browser; 400,000 members have downloaded it since. CompuServe, AOL and Delphi all plan to add millions of users to the Web later this year. And this August when Microsoft ships its Windows 95 software, another 20 million to 30 million could be one click away from the Internet. Its Microsoft Network and one-button Internet access will be packaged with the new operating software. . . .

Ann Arbor, Mich., consultant Joel Maloff, who tracks Net activity, estimated Internet access revenue at about $47 million in 1993. Last year, that grew to $120 million. He had estimated this year's revenues to hit $300 million; now, he says it will reach $540 million.

Throw in the commercial services and the U.S. market alone will top $1 billion, Maloff says. . . .

About the network's evolution, Stephen Wolff, formerly in charge of the National Science Foundation's NSFNet network, says, "I don't really go along with the notion that we have something here that will revolutionize society. . . . I think it has real promises for participative government and demonstrating real results for people in business. It ain't revolution, but it's really big stuff." ■

Opening day at the easyEverything Internet cafe in Times Square, New York City, November 28, 2000. *Chris Hondros/ Newsmakers/Getty Images*

Sam Ward/USA TODAY

OUTSOURCING

USA's new money-saving export: White-collar jobs

By Stephanie Armour and Michelle Kessler
Excerpt from article published August 5, 2003

White-collar employees have long believed their jobs were safe from the economic forces that have shifted millions of factory jobs to foreign countries in the last 30 years.

Not anymore.

It's not just clothing and electronics being made by workers in India, China and similar places. Now, office and professional jobs are being shipped out — raising the specter that skilled white-collar workers could face the same devastating job losses that decimated the manufacturing industry.

Almost any professional job that can be done long-distance is suddenly up for grabs. Jobs done by financial analysts, architectural drafters, telemarketers, accountants, claims adjusters, home loan processors and others at higher levels of the labor food chain are being farmed out to workers in other countries.

"We're not just talking about call-center jobs, but all kinds of jobs," says Deloitte Consulting analyst Christopher Gentle. "It doesn't leave any part of the corporation untouched." . . . ■

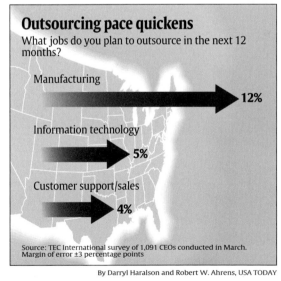

Published March 22, 2004

Outsourcing pace quickens
What jobs do you plan to outsource in the next 12 months?

Manufacturing — 12%

Information technology — 5%

Customer support/sales — 4%

Source: TEC International survey of 1,091 CEOs conducted in March. Margin of error ±3 percentage points

By Darryl Haralson and Robert W. Ahrens, USA TODAY

Workers asked to train foreign replacements

By Stephanie Armour

Excerpt from article published April 6, 2004

When computer programmer Stephen Gentry learned last year that Boeing was laying him off and shipping his job overseas, he wasn't too surprised. Many of his friends had suffered the same experience.

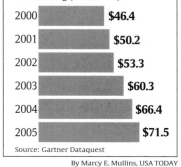

Created November 18, 2002

Outsourcing leap

Businesses and government agencies are expected to spend more on outsourcing (in billions):

2000	$46.4
2001	$50.2
2002	$53.3
2003	$60.3
2004	$66.4
2005	$71.5

Source: Gartner Dataquest

By Marcy E. Mullins, USA TODAY

What really stunned him was his last assignment: Managers had him train the worker from India who'd be taking his job.

"It was very callous," says Gentry, 51, of Auburn, Wash., a father of three who is still unemployed. "They asked us to make them feel at home while we trained them to take our jobs."

More cost-cutting companies are hiring workers in other countries to do jobs formerly held by U.S. employees. But in a painful twist, some employers are asking the workers they're laying off to train their foreign replacements — having them dig their own unemployment graves.

Almost one in five information technology workers has lost a job or knows someone who lost a job after training a foreign worker, according to a new survey by the Washington Alliance of Technology Workers. The study is the first to quantify how widespread the practice is.

Here's what typically happens: U.S. workers getting pink slips are told they can get another paycheck or beefed-up severance if they're willing to teach workers from India, China and other countries how to do their jobs. The foreign workers typically arrive for a few weeks or months of training. When they leave, they take U.S. jobs with them. The U.S. employees who trained them are then laid off. . . . ■

Stop Exporting American Jobs

Union workers hold signs during a rally against outsourcing, March 5, 2004, on Capitol Hill in Washington, D.C. *Mark Wilson/Getty Images*

AN EXPANDED
SPORTS ROSTER

Live action during the NASCAR Crown Royal 400 at
Richmond International Raceway, May 6, 2006.
Sean Dougherty/USA TODAY

NASCAR sets fast pace

By Steve Ballard
Excerpt from article published January 16, 1997

It stands to reason that a sport predicated on speed would arrive at the next century a few years early.

Riding a comet adorned with NASCAR Winston Cup decals, auto racing is hurtling into 1997 with no stop sign in sight.

Not so long ago labeled as a sport for the very rich, watched only by the very bored, motor sports — be it cars, trucks, boats or snowmobiles — is running circles around many of its sporting brethren.

At a time when more traditional pastimes are measuring success by TV ratings and attendance that didn't dip as much this year as last, motor sports is hustling to print tickets fast enough.

So why this relatively sudden boom? Theories abound, with the most prevalent pointing to the astronomical salaries, labor unrest, high ticket prices and general incivility that have come to characterize pro sports in the 1990s.

But Rick Hendrick, whose teams have won the last two Winston Cup championships, prefers to believe motor sports earned its way onto center stage more by its thrills than the rest of sporting society's ills. "We're the last of the gladiator sports," he says. "It's competitive, it's dangerous, it's exciting."

Dale Earnhardt, photographed here on February 13, 1997, was 49 years old when he was killed in a crash at the 2001 Daytona 500. A seventime Winston Cup champ, Earnhardt was one of NASCAR's most prominent stars.
AP Images

And it's expanding.

Motor sports, with Bruton Smith at the forefront, has turned the fantasy of "build it and they will come" into a multimillion-dollar reality. . . .

"Maybe 15 years ago we were a redneck sport, although I don't know what that is. Maybe I'm one," Smith says. "To me, it sounds derogatory, so let's suppose instead that we were a blue-collar sport. Well, we're no longer that today.

"The factory workers still come, but so does management and the guy who owns the factory. They're all coming. And they all bring their wives." . . . ■

Ricky Craven (41) flips into the catchfence in Turn 1 of the Talladega Superspeedway during the Winston Select 500 on Sunday, April 28, 1996. Also visible are Derrike Cope (12), Geoff Bodine (7), Brett Bodine (11), and Mark Martin (6). *AP Images*

Snowboarder Shaun White competes during the men's snowboard halfpipe finals of the 2006 Winter Olympics. White, nicknamed "The Flying Tomato," is also a skateboarding star and an X Games regular.
Joe Klamar/AFP/Getty Images

STEPPING OUT OF THE CLOSET

Same-sex couples from San Francisco dance during a marriage equality rally on October 11, 2004, in Washington, D.C. *Alex Wong/Getty Images*

SURGING HISPANIC POPULATION

Por Un Barrio Mejor
ILGWU

UNION MADE ILGWU

ABAJO CON LA EXPLOTACION
A NUESTRA CLASE OBRERA

A young child and a woman walk past a wall mural September 22, 2003, in Chicago's mainly Hispanic Little Village neighborhood. *Tim Boyle/Getty Images*

U.S.-born Hispanics propel growth

By Haya El Nasser

Excerpt from article published May 10, 2006

Hispanics remain the USA's fastest-growing minority group, but most of their population increase comes from births here rather than immigration, according to Census Bureau estimates released Tuesday.

As debate over immigration policy roils the nation, government numbers show that 60% of the 1.3 million new Hispanics in 2005 are citizens because they were born here.

"When all the attention is on immigration, natural increase is what's driving the population change," says Roberto Suro, director of the Pew Hispanic Center.

A third of the nation's 296.4 million people are considered minorities. Hispanics are the largest minority group at 42.7 million, up 3.3% from mid-2004 to mid-2005. The Census counts all residents and makes no distinction between those here legally and illegally. The Pew Center estimates that up to 12 million U.S. residents are undocumented, most of them Hispanic.

William Frey, demographer at the Brookings Institution, says one of every two new Americans every year is Hispanic.

"Hispanics are here, and they're part of our future, and they're a large part of our young population," he says. "They're a part of America because they're born in America." . . . ■

Published August 7, 2005

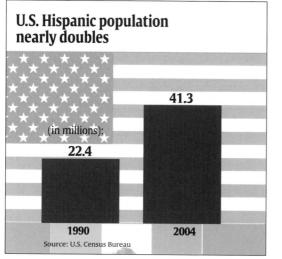

U.S. Hispanic population nearly doubles

(in millions):

22.4 — 1990
41.3 — 2004

Source: U.S. Census Bureau

By David Stuckey and Keith Simmons, USA TODAY

Second graders line up with their books after language arts class in Oasis, California, on Monday, October 18, 2004. More than 90 percent of the school's students are Hispanic. They are taught only in English — still a foreign language for many. *AP Images*

REALITY TV TAKES OFF

Survivor finale hits ratings high

By Gary Levin

Excerpted from article published August 25, 2000

An average of almost 52 million people saw the two-hour finale of CBS' *Survivor* Wednesday, the most-watched program this year other than the Super Bowl.

The figure, from Nielsen Media Research, far exceeded projections and easily beat the Academy Awards telecast, which usually ranks second each year. This year's Oscars broadcast drew 46.3 million viewers March 26. The Super Bowl drew 88.5 million.

Survivor's audience grew 85% from last week. The episode also gained nearly 15 million viewers between its 8 p.m. ET starting time and the final half-hour beginning at 9:30, when 58.6 million were tuned in to see Richard Hatch, 39, a corporate trainer from Newport, R.I., win the $1 million prize. . . . ■

OPPOSITE: Ozzy, Sharon, Jack and Kelly Osbourne starred in *The Osbournes*, which ran from 2002 to 2005. "You know who wrote the script? God," said Ozzy. *Michael Yarish/MTV/Getty Images*

RIGHT: Elisabeth Filarski (now Hasselbeck) competes in a challenge in *Survivor: The Australian Outback*. She later married NFL quarterback Matt Hasselbeck and became a co-host of *The View. Monty Brinton/CBS Photo Archive/Getty Images*

ABOVE TOP: Nicole Richie and Paris Hilton of *The Simple Life* at the Fox Studios in Los Angeles in June 2004. *Dan MacMedan/USA Today*

ABOVE BOTTOM: Donald Trump of *The Apprentice* at the Emmy Awards in 2005. *Dan MacMedan/USA TODAY*

In reality, TV has been pretty good this year

By Robert Bianco

Excerpted from article published December 26, 2000

Reality. Can we escape the concept?

Not any time soon, I fear — no matter how exhausted we all may be after a TV year dominated by reality in all its facets, from games to electoral gambits. It seems we spent half our time just watching people count votes, from Palm Beach to Pulau Tiga.

Like it or not, the reality trend is not abating. The stratospheric success of the year's two most popular reality series, *Who Wants to Be a Millionaire* and *Survivor*, would be more than enough to guarantee a continued onslaught of shows placing real people in contrived situations. . . . ■

TV viewers idolize reality

By Gary Levin
Excerpted from article published April 14, 2004

Reality shows are among the most popular this season: Three of them — *American Idol, Survivor* and *The Apprentice* — rank in TV's top 5, and they've even eclipsed the departing *Friends* as subjects for water-cooler chat.

A sampling appears to the right. (Fox's limited-run *My Big Fat Obnoxious Fiance* and *The Simple Life* are among other stand-outs.) ... □

Kelly Clarkson, the first winner of *American Idol,* competes on the show in 2002.
Robert Hanashiro/ USA TODAY

Viewers (in millions)

American Idol (Fox) 25.6

Survivor: All-Stars (CBS) 22.4

Apprentice (NBC) 19.6

Fear Factor (NBC) 13.9

Bachelorette (ABC) 11.6

Avg. Joe: Hawaii (NBC) 11.1

Extreme Makeover (ABC) 11.1

CONNECTED THROUGH TECHNOLOGY

Cellular phones on the move

By Mark Lewyn
Excerpt from article published October 14, 1987

Without cellular phones, says Charles Hard, his small tugboat business in Houston would be up a creek. . . .

"It's an essential part of my business," says the 47-year-old co-owner of Hard's Marine Service Inc., who racks up $1,500 in phone bills a month. "The only thing I have against it really is that it's pretty expensive."

True, but that's changing. Despite high costs and a significant rate of customers who have dropped the service — an estimated 30% a year — cellular phones are selling in record numbers. And the Cellular Telecommunications Industry Association projects that somewhere cellular phone No. 1 million will go into use today.

Not bad, considering that cellular phones have been around since Oct. 13, 1983. That's when Ameritech — one of the seven regional Bell operating companies — started the first system in Chicago.

So far, most sales have been to business people for business purposes.

For good reason. Cellular phones are hardly cheap: It costs $1,000 to $1,300 to buy a phone, a fixed rate of $25 to $50 a month, and 35 to 50 cents per calling minute. . . . ■

Motorola director of systems engineering Ray Leopold holds an early cellular phone, June 26, 1990.
AP Images

Surge in text messaging
makes cell operators :-)

By Kevin Maney
Excerpt from article published July 28, 2005

It takes the number of characters in this paragraph — just 160 — to flirt, avoid traffic jams, balance your checking accounts, help Africa and win a generation.

Text messaging on cellphones is finally taking off in the USA. It has been around for years and is a huge part of life in Japan and South Korea. But in the U.S. market, text messaging had caught on only among teens and *American Idol* fans voting for their favorites — until the past year or so. . . .

About 5 billion text messages are sent a month in the USA, up from 2.8 billion a year ago, according to the wireless trade association CTIA. But the real story is in the inventive ways this medium is being used and penetrating everyday life. . . . ■

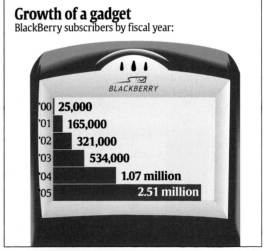

Published June 16, 2003

Texting on the rise
U.S. mobile text messages sent:

1 billion

252 million

14.4 million

| December 2000 | December 2001 | December 2002 |

Source: Cellular Telecommunications & Internet Association

By Suzy Parker, USA TODAY

Growth of PDA injuries
a concern for companies

By Stephanie Armour
Excerpt from article published November 10, 2006

Employment lawyers are warning companies they could face liability or workers' compensation claims related to employee injuries from personal digital assistants.

The American Physical Therapy Association in Alexandria, Va., and other occupational organizations warn that improper use and overuse of personal digital assistants (PDAs) can lead to hand throbbing, tendonitis and swelling, a condition known as BlackBerry Thumb, named after the popular PDA. . . .

Some hotels catering to business clients offer treatments for the problem. The Hyatt Regency Scottsdale Resort and Spa in Scottsdale, Ariz., offers a special BlackBerry Balm Hand Massage that runs $80 for 30 minutes. A resort spokeswoman says the treatment has become very popular. . . . ■

Published April 24, 2006

Growth of a gadget
BlackBerry subscribers by fiscal year:

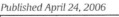

'00	25,000
'01	165,000
'02	321,000
'03	534,000
'04	1.07 million
'05	2.51 million

Source: Research In Motion   By David Stuckey and Adrienne Lewis, USA TODAY

PART FOUR
25 AMERICANS

Lance Armstrong
Graham Chadwick/Getty Images

25 AMERICANS WHO SHAPE OUR LIVES

Influence and inspiration from the most unlikely of sources can shape our lives. Consider the college dropouts who have pushed the desktop revolution, changing how we work, shop and play; the athlete who conquered cancer and then conquered his sport; the teenager in Indiana who taught us about courage and compassion; or the cartoonist who created Bart, Homer and the rest of the Simpsons.

Few have had more impact on our lives than the presidents who have governed our nation, but we left them off the list because their influence goes without saying. Americans who we considered but did not include form a who's who of politics, art, industry and entertainment: Nancy Pelosi, Rupert Murdoch, Colin Powell, George Lucas, Stephen King, Kurt Cobain and many, many others who have shaped our nation in ways obvious or subtle.

This list of 25 Americans is a snapshot of our nation over the past quarter century. It gives a sense of how we have changed and why we have changed, and also, perhaps, gives us a glimpse of what is to come over the next 25 years.

Lance Armstrong
Inspiration on wheels

Lance Armstrong was 25 years old and one of the best cyclists in the world when he was diagnosed with testicular cancer in 1996. Doctors told Armstrong that the disease might be fatal, but after three years of intensive chemotherapy, surgery and recuperation, Armstrong was ready to compete again. Armstrong won his first Tour de France in 1999 and then won it again every year until 2005, the longest streak of wins in the history of the Tour.

Armstrong's recovery and Tour triumphs made him a source of inspiration and courage. He told USA TODAY in 2002, "It's not a burden, and I'll do it until they ask me not to. Someday there might be a 15-year-old girl who won't know or care who Lance Armstrong is, and someone else can step in and be her inspiration. Until then, I'll try to meet every request, every person who can use some help."

And those ubiquitous yellow Livestrong bracelets? The Lance Armstrong Foundation has raised more than $60 million through their sales.

Garth Brooks
Mainstream cowboy

In 1985, Garth Brooks headed to Nashville. "I spent 23 hours there and ran back home," he said. He went back in 1987, and this time he stayed.

His second album, *No Fences*, hit it big in 1990, and his music was everywhere. With Brooks leading the charge, country radio was booming and album sales peaked.

Throughout the 1990s Brooks was more than just a huge star in a niche genre: he was a huge star, period. Songs like "The Dance," "Friends in Low Places" and "The Thunder Rolls" made him a household name. When he played a free concert in New York City in 1997, the parks department estimated the crowd at 1.1 million.

One key to Brooks' crossover appeal is that his musical influences are varied: He admires Janis Joplin, Billy Joel and even KISS. He told USA WEEKEND in 1992 that where music is headed, "there won't be country music, there won't be rap music, all the labels. It'll just be what sounds good and feels good to people. That's what they'll listen to, and the rest will fall by the wayside."

Ellen DeGeneres
TV pioneer

In 1997, Ellen DeGeneres made headlines and history by announcing the character she played on her hit TV show, *Ellen*, was a lesbian — and that the

Ellen DeGeneres
Frederick M. Brown/Getty Images

same was true for the actress in real life. Although the TV landscape in 1997 had numerous gay characters in supporting roles, she became TV's first gay lead character, provoking cheers from some and outrage from others.

A New Orleans native, DeGeneres got her first big break in 1986, when she appeared on *The Tonight Show*. She earned some small roles after that, but it was *Ellen*, which debuted in 1994, that put her career in high gear. The show's original title was *These Friends of Mine*, but as the show's focus shifted to DeGeneres' character, the show's title changed as well.

Although *Ellen* was canceled the year after the coming-out episode, DeGeneres found subsequent success with a daytime talk show and as a host of the Oscars and Emmys. At the 2001 Emmys, which had been twice delayed due to 9/11, Ellen famously quipped, "What would bug the Taliban more than seeing a gay woman, in a suit, surrounded by Jews?"

Garth Brooks
*Mario Ruiz/Time Life
Pictures/Getty Images*

Jerry Falwell
Web Bryant/USA TODAY

Jerry Falwell
Founding father of the religious right

Rev. Jerry Falwell founded Moral Majority in 1979, leading the charge of conservative religious leaders into U.S. politics. Falwell, who died in 2007, also helmed PTL ministry after Jim Bakker left PTL in disgrace, beamed *Old Time Gospel Hour* to hundreds of TV stations and founded Liberty University.

He often drew attention for remarks that some found outrageous, but his impact on America is nothing to dismiss. As USA TODAY noted in 2007, "The Moral Majority was groundbreaking, even revolutionary. It sought an activist role for fundamentalists who had seen politics as something to be avoided."

In an interview with USA TODAY in 1987, Falwell assessed his organization's impact: "We have been able to achieve the involvement of conservative, religious Americans, who were heretofore disenfranchised citizens. We have been able to inform and mobilize thousands of conservative pastors. . . . Today, the evangelical and fundamentalist churches have done exactly what the black church did 30 years ago. They have thrown their hats into the ring and will never leave."

Bill Gates
Software titan

In 1975, Bill Gates left Harvard during his junior year to found Microsoft Corporation with his childhood friend, Paul Allen. They shared a bold vision of "a computer on every desk and in every home" — all running Microsoft software. And their vision almost came true. Today, Microsoft's signature software, Windows, is used on nine out of 10 desktop PCs. But Microsoft's reach extends much further than Windows. Its Office software is as common as Windows, and it has ventured into hardware, video games, e-mail and more.

Bill Gates
Robert Hanashiro/USA TODAY

Gates announced in 2006 that he would relinquish his duties as chief software architect. Philanthropy is Gates' new focus. The Bill & Melinda Gates Foundation has almost $30 billion in assets, and has made a mark fighting AIDS and through other global health and learning initiatives. In addition to the foundation's assets, Gates plans to give away most of his personal wealth, which is estimated at upwards of $50 billion. As USA TODAY noted in 2006, "he could become the greatest philanthropist ever." Not bad for a college dropout.

Newt Gingrich
Architect of the Republican revolution

In 1994, Newt Gingrich engineered a sweeping Republican takeover of Congress, keyed by his Contract with America. The Contract, which was signed by many of the Republicans running for office that year, called for a balanced budget amendment, middle-class and capital-gains tax cuts, a defense buildup and tough crime and welfare bills. It was, according to USA TODAY, "politically brilliant."

Newt Gingrich
Tim Dillon/USA TODAY

The results on election day were dramatic: Republicans gained 52 House seats and eight Senate seats. It was the first time in 40 years that Republicans controlled the House. Shortly after the election, Gingrich was installed as Speaker.

Gingrich was a polarizing figure: "I am the most serious, systematic revolutionary of modern times," he said in 1994. He left office in 1998 and has stayed busy an author and speaker.

Al Gore
Global warming gadfly

On December 13, 2000, Al Gore conceded the presidential election to George W. Bush. Six years later, Gore stood on stage and accepted an Oscar for *An Inconvenient Truth*, his global warming documentary.

The documentary helped bring renewed attention to global warming. "We do not have time to play around with this," Gore warned members of the House science and energy committees in March 2007, calling the situation a "planetary emergency."

Although vocal skeptics exist, government at all levels and corporate America are increasingly embracing the idea of reducing the human contribution to global warming.

Gore's environment crusade has deep roots. He wrote *Earth in the Balance* in 1989 "to communicate the true nature of the global environmental crisis." *An Inconvenient Truth* had its origins in a slide show that Gore developed and gave for years prior to the film being made. He continues to travel the world presenting the slide show.

Al Gore
Robert Hanashiro/USA TODAY

Alan Greenspan

The central banker

Alan Greenspan
H. Darr Beiser/USA TODAY

As chair of the Federal Reserve, Alan Greenspan held the reins of the U.S. economy from 1987 until his retirement in 2006. During his tenure, the economy enjoyed a 10-year economic expansion — the longest in history — and had just two brief recessions that were the mildest since World War II.

Greenspan once dreamed of being a baseball player and toured the country playing clarinet in a swing band. But even then he would read finance books between sets. He returned to school and earned a master's degree in 1950, and then launched a career that brought him to the pinnacle of finance. Upon his retirement, he was lauded as perhaps the greatest central banker ever.

Greenspan's success at the Fed earned him a larger-than-life, oracle-like persona. But he never lost his sense of humor.

He once famously said: "Since I've become a central banker, I've learned to mumble with great incoherence. If I seem unduly clear to you, you must have misunderstood what I said."

Matt Groening

Homer's creator

Matt Groening
Frazer Harrison/Getty Images

When *The Simpsons* first hit the air in 1989, USA TODAY called the new series a gift. Today, it's a gift that keeps on giving. The Simpsons has aired over 400 episodes, spawned a movie and is a syndication dynamo. The show was Fox's first big hit and led to a flurry of prime-time cartoons aimed at adults, including *King of the Hill*, *Family Guy* and *South Park*.

"I love the style that we stumbled into, this high-velocity pacing that allowed us to do every kind of comedy we could think of, from the most high-falutin' literary references to sub-*Three Stooges* physical abuse," series creator Matt Groening said.

An Oregon native, Groening was a writer for an alternative L.A. newspaper when he created a comic strip he called *Life in Hell*. It drew the attention of a producer from *The Tracy Ullman Show*, and Groening created the Simpson family to fill one-minute interludes on Ullman's show.

Has *The Simpsons* slipped over the years? Not in Groening's opinion. It's as "smart and twisted" as ever, he says.

Jesse Jackson
America's vocal minority

When Rev. Jesse Jackson was a boy growing up in Greenville, South Carolina, his family shared an outhouse with another family. Chain gangs would come and clean the streets. There were parks he couldn't go to and benches he couldn't sit on because he was black. "I like to think that you get your stars from your scars," Jackson says.

Jackson overcame his humble beginning, working as an aide to Martin Luther King, Jr., before starting his own organization, Operation PUSH, in 1971. In 1984 and 1988 he ran for president. A 1987 profile in USA TODAY called him a "Baptist preacher, civil rights leader, self-appointed diplomat, gadfly politician, the most visible and outspoken black in America."

Although his profile isn't as high today as it was when he was running for president, Jackson remains visible, appearing around the country and the world as an advocate for various causes.

Jesse Jackson
Paul T. Whyte/USA TODAY

Steve Jobs
Apple's visionary

The fiercely private Steve Jobs was once asked if he would ever write an autobiography. "I've thought about it a lot," he said, "but it would take 1½ to 2 years. And what I really care about most is making great products."

Jobs, a college dropout who co-founded Apple in 1976, has a long track record of creating remarkable products. In 1984, Apple produced the Macintosh. The Mac revolutionized the personal computer industry. Its operating system was remarkably easy to use and intuitive, eliminating the need to type in DOS commands.

But in 1985, Jobs was forced out at Apple. "His tenure was marked by brilliance in the early days but turmoil as the start-up struggled to become a midsize, professionally managed company. He ran Apple like a religion, not a business," USA TODAY wrote in 1997.

Jobs rebounded quickly, buying film company Pixar for $10 million. Then in 1997, a desperate Apple, which had lost $1.7 billion in the previous seven quarters, turned to Jobs to save the company. Back in charge, his impact was felt quickly. Jobs introduced the iMac in 1998, the iPod in 2001 and the iPhone in 2006 — all products he no doubt considers great.

Steve Jobs
Diana Walker/Liaison/Getty Images

Michael Jordan
Rare air

The greatest player in the history of his game and legend the world over, Michael Jordan led the Chicago Bulls to six NBA championships. He was the worldwide face of the game — as well as the face of the various sneakers, cars, hamburgers, underwear and long distance phone plans that he endorsed.

And he became an icon. "Baggy shorts. The shaved head. The wagging tongue. The smile. Michael Jordan's mannerisms have become almost as much a part of pop culture as Elvis' sneer," wrote USA TODAY in 1996. At the peak of his celebrity, Jordan was so revered that an interviewer from USA TODAY asked, "What does it feel like to hear people say, 'Michael Jordan is God'?" Jordan's response: "It's very embarrassing, because I see myself as an athlete who plays a sport, for enjoyment and entertainment to others."

Jordan retired and unretired twice before calling it quits for good in 2003. In his last season he chalked up one more record, becoming the only man over 40 years of age to score 40 points in a game.

Rush Limbaugh
The loudest man on talk radio

Rush Limbaugh first hit the national airwaves in 1988, and his success was rapid. He led the charge of conservative radio hosts who quickly gained unprecedented power, beaming their voices — and opinions — into the daily lives of millions of Americans.

Rush Limbaugh
AP Images

Limbaugh has seen his share of controversies and has been criticized for, among other things, contributing to the polarization of politics: "Militant feminists are 'femi-Nazis'; gay activist groups represent 'the New McCarthyism'; the green movement and animal rights groups are riddled with wackos, socialists and communist sympathizers; [and] the Greenhouse Effect is a myth," USA TODAY wrote in 1992 about some of Limbaugh's on-air positions.

But to Limbaugh, his show is about entertainment. It mixes politics with music and humor. "If the show wasn't fun, I wouldn't have half the audience I have now," he said in 1992.

Michael Jordan
AP Images

Madonna
Jo Hale/Getty Images

Madonna

Pop icon

Madonna, born Madonna Louise Veronica Ciccone, grew up in Pontiac and Rochester, Michigan. Her teen years were rebellious. High school "was painful in a way," she told USA WEEKEND. "The idea that I had a dream or a goal made me feel strong, superior, so when people didn't smile at me, I didn't care. I was going to be somebody."

And she did become somebody: Her hits include "Material Girl," "Like a Virgin," "Papa Don't Preach" and "Like a Prayer." She's starred in movies — *Evita* and *Dick Tracy*, among others. And she became "the planet's most notorious icon," according to a 1992 article in USA TODAY, pushing boundaries with a sex-soaked persona.

Madonna's self-titled first album appeared in 1983. What's been the secret to her staying power? "To have longevity, you have to be willing to constantly challenge yourself to deliver something new. You have to change and grow, to evolve, to be a reflection of what's going on in the world."

Sandra Day O'Connor

The swing vote

Sandra Day O'Connor entered the Supreme Court as its first woman justice. She became the pivotal swing vote, the key bridge between the left and right wings of the court. In 2000, USA TODAY described her as "a conservative with an asterisk: a pragmatic jurist who, when she sees fit, will vote with the four liberal justices." On abortion, affirmative action, voting rights, sexual harassment, states' rights and more, O'Connor played a leading role in shaping Supreme Court decisions.

Sandra Day O'Connor
AP Images

Prior to joining the head court, she was the first woman majority leader of the Arizona state Senate and a judge on the Arizona Court of Appeals. Ronald Reagan appointed O'Connor to the Supreme Court in 1981, and she was unanimously confirmed.

O'Connor has scarcely slowed down since leaving the court. In a 2006 interview with USA TODAY, she was asked how retirement suited her. "I need to retire from retirement. I'm too busy!" was her response.

Howard Schultz
The king of coffee

Howard Schultz
Toru Yamanaka/AFP/Getty Images

A story in USA WEEKEND in 1997 said it all: "Howard Schultz is the Bill Gates of coffee." In 1982, Schultz accepted a job as head of sales and marketing at Starbucks, then a chain of four Seattle coffee shops. In 1987, he purchased the company, becoming president and CEO at the age of 33. Schultz, who was raised in a Brooklyn housing project, has led Starbucks through incredible expansion.

Shultz says the key to Starbucks' growth is its values. His father, a cabby, "was a bitter man because the system devalued him. At Starbucks, I wanted to make sure we were respectful of people's lives." In an interview with USA TODAY, Schultz said, "We're living in a time where the consumer is doing something they've never done before. They're performing their own audit, a cultural audit of what a company stands for."

What does the future hold for Starbucks? The company accounts for less than 1% of international coffee consumption, Shultz noted in 2003. "These are still the early days in the growth and development of Starbucks."

Russell Simmons
The godfather of hip-hop

Russell Simmons
Todd Plitt/USA TODAY

Russell Simmons was one of the early pioneers of hip-hop — not as a rapper, but as a businessman. Simmons co-founded one of the first successful rap record labels, Def Jam Records, in 1984. Run-DMC, Beastie Boys, Public Enemy and LL Cool J all got their start with Def Jam. Simmons told USA TODAY in 2000 that "we made a record company because the artists needed a record company, and no one respected their work."

USA TODAY wrote in 2007 that "Simmons' world is one where the vibe of the streets can be cleaned up — a bit — and sold to the masses." Simmons' reach extends well beyond music. He founded Phat Farm, the first successful "urban clothing" company, and he is also involved in a variety of other business ventures, including TV and movie production and even a Broadway show.

Simmons is not the stereotypical mogul. He is a vegan and is obsessed with yoga, about which he says "Yoga takes me to a place that's mystical, whether it's Nirvana or Christian consciousness."

Steven Spielberg
America's favorite director

Steven Spielberg directed his first feature-length film when he was 16. *Firefly* was about aliens who abducted humans for an extraterrestrial zoo. His mother helped with the special effects, throwing cherries in syrup all over her kitchen cabinets.

Spielberg has come a long way since those humble beginnings. *Jaws*, *Close Encounters of the Third Kind*, *E.T.*, the *Indiana Jones* franchise, *The Color Purple*, *Jurassic Park*, *Schindler's List*, *Saving Private Ryan* and *War of the Worlds* are just some of the movies that have made him the most popular filmmaker of our time. Spielberg has also been the producer or executive producer of numerous other movies, including *Back to the Future* and *Gremlins*.

Spielberg has used his fame and fortune to set up a foundation to record the testimony of Holocaust survivors. The director, who has seven kids and a stepdaughter, also has a less serious side. He collects movie memorabilia and loves to play video games — "I play them on the set, at home or at the office between meetings."

Steven Spielberg
Robert Hanashiro/USA TODAY

Martha Stewart
America's lifestyle expert

Entertainment guru Martha Stewart presides over a media and merchandising empire. She has made her mark with TV shows, cookbooks, magazines and merchandise. USA TODAY wrote in 2000 that she "intuits what women dream about: a beautiful, organized home and garden; great food; style; and the skills and products to pull it all off."

Stewart is the long-reigning queen of lifestyle advice. She released her first book, *Entertaining*, in 1982, launched *Martha Stewart Living* magazine in 1990, and started her syndicated TV show in 1993. Even a brief prison sentence related to a questionable stock sale wasn't able to derail Stewart, who called it "an unwelcome interruption."

One of the secrets to Stewart's success is no secret at all: hard work. In 1989, Stewart told USA TODAY, "I work more hours than anyone else I know. I don't sleep and I'm tired lots of times, but I still will take the time to gild a pumpkin, to marbleize a Christmas ornament."

Martha Stewart
Eileen Blass/USA TODAY

Ted Turner
Ted Thai/Time Life Pictures/Getty Images

Ted Turner
Cable pioneer

"Ted Turner isn't afraid to go anywhere. In his Ford Taurus. In his private jet. And especially in his brain," USA TODAY wrote in 2000. When Turner launched CNN — the first 24-hour, all-news network — in 1980, it seemed like an off-the-wall idea. He also launched a number of other cable stations, started the Goodwill Games, pledged $1 billion to the United Nations and, due to his sprawling bison ranches, became America's largest individual landowner.

Turner has been called "The Mouth of the South" and "Captain Outrageous." But as his son, Beau, told USA TODAY in 2000, "Now, you may think he's a dumb redneck. But . . . if you underestimate him, you're a fool."

In 2000, Ted Turner confessed to USA TODAY that he does have at least one weakness: "After having done CNN and Superstation, winning the America's Cup in 1977 and the '95 World Series with the Atlanta Braves, I feel that I can do just about anything. Except have a successful marriage. But I've tried. At least, I'm still trying."

J. Craig Venter
Mapper of the human genome

According to a profile published in USA TODAY in 2000: "For the past 10 years, J. Craig Venter, 53, has been perhaps the most vilified scientist in the world." His methods for unraveling the genetic code were controversial, but Venter persevered — and triumphed. His scientific team at Celera Genomics assembled the first whole genome of a human being, making a joint announcement with the publicly funded Human Genome Project at the White House in 2000.

J. Craig Venter
Tim Dillon/USA TODAY

Perhaps Venter's sailing background was good practice for weathering controversy: Before being consumed by the genome project, Venter was an avid and fearless sailor, and survived several life-threatening storms at sea.

What are the ramifications of mapping the human genome? "Such a map is a Holy Grail of modern science, a key to 21st century advances that could turn many common diseases into bad memories," wrote USA WEEKEND in 1999. Bill Clinton, at the White House announcement, put it more poetically: "Our children may know cancer only as a constellation of stars."

Sam Walton
Retail giant

Sam Walton
Diana Walker/Time Life Pictures/Getty Images

Sam Walton opened the nation's first Wal-Mart in 1962. He was 44 and had already spent over 20 years in a retail career that started as a J.C. Penney management trainee. By the time Walton died in 1992, over 1,700 Wal-Mart stores were open for business, along with numerous Sam's Clubs. USA TODAY noted at the time that Walton had "become a billionaire, won the nation's highest civilian honor — and changed the rules of retailing forever."

Along the way Walton became famous for his frugality. "Mr. Sam," USA TODAY noted, "was famous for driving a pickup instead of riding in a limousine. His ground-floor office . . . looks out over a parking lot and looks as though it was decorated out of his store aisles: fake wood paneling, formica desk."

In his autobiography, Walton listed his rules for building a business: "Rule 1: Commit to your business. I think I overcame every single one of my personal shortcomings by the sheer passion I brought to my work."

Ryan White
An early face of AIDS

Ryan White
Kim Komenich/Time Life Pictures/Getty Images

When Ryan White was diagnosed with AIDS in December 1984, he was a seventh grader living in Kokomo, Indiana. He collected GI Joe toys and comic books, and after his diagnosis he was eager to get back to school. But White — who contracted AIDS through a blood transfusion — was not allowed to return to Western Middle School. Fear of AIDS was rampant, and as White fought to live as normal a life as possible he became a national spokesman for others with the disease.

Ryan eventually won the right to go to school. The Whites moved to Cicero, Indiana, where he was welcomed at Hamilton Heights High School. "I'm just one of the kids, and all because the students . . . listened to the facts, educated their parents and themselves and believed in me," White said. White spoke often to children about AIDS. "I don't want anyone to go through what I went through," he would say.

Ryan White died April 8, 1990, at the age of 18. "For everyone out there who learns to hate, someone out there learns to care because of Ryan," said U.S. Surgeon General Antonia Novello.

Oprah Winfrey

The queen of talk

Oprah Winfrey began her career as a 17-year-old radio reporter in Nashville, moving to television two years later. By the age of 24 she was traveling regularly to Hollywood to interview the stars. In 1985 Winfrey hit the big screen herself, playing Sofia in the movie *The Color Purple*. *The Oprah Winfrey Show* went into syndication on 128 stations the following year, and by 1987 Winfrey's show topped the genre.

Oprah is more than a talk show host. She "has emerged as a spiritual leader for the new millennium, a moral voice of authority for the nation. With her television pulpit and the sheer power of her persona, she has encouraged and steered audiences (mostly women) in all matters, from genocide in Rwanda to suburban spouse swapping to finding the absolute best T-shirt and oatmeal cookie," wrote USA TODAY in 2006.

Winfrey grew up poor on a farm in rural Mississippi. According to *Forbes* magazine, she now has an estimated wealth of $1.5 billion, making her the richest African American in the world and the richest self-made woman in America.

Oprah Winfrey, with Bob Hope
AP Images

Tiger Woods

A new kind of golfer

Tiger Woods is unquestionably the best male golfer of his generation, having won 12 majors as of 2007. His success on the PGA Tour and his endorsement deals with Nike, General Mills, American Express and others have made him an icon.

In the world of golf, the multiracial Woods has shattered the color barrier. Woods has credited his success to the mentoring and support of his father, Earl Woods, a former Green Beret who was the first African American to play baseball in the Big 12 collegiate conference. "I don't consider people like Jack Nicklaus as heroes," Tiger Woods told USA TODAY for a 1992 story headlined "Golf's Next Star." "I admire them for their golf. I guess my role model is my dad."

Woods was a child golf prodigy, winning a children's pitch-putt-and-drive contest at the age of two. In his first television interview, at the age of three, he revealed the secret to his success: "pwactice."

Tiger Woods
Eileen Blass/USA TODAY

A man stands in front of a makeshift memorial on the campus of Virginia Tech on April 18, 2007. *Charles Ommanney/Getty Images*

Alabama farmer Ben Cosby looks skyward with thanks as nearly two inches of rain falls on his cotton field on June 17, 1988, following a record-breaking drought. *AP Images*

A young girl stands in a hallway in the City of God orphanage in Port-au-Prince, Haiti, on June 2, 2004. *Jack Gruber/USA TODAY*

U.S. Army Capt. Todd Kelly talks on the radio in the darkened main hall of Baghdad's Presidential Palace in Iraq on April 7, 2003. *Jack Gruber/USA Today*

Boats at a New Orleans marina after Hurricane Katrina, which devastated the region on August 29, 2005. *Brian Snyder-Pool/Getty Images*

A fisherman rests in his boat off the coast of Indonesian village Lambada Lhok, which was destroyed following the massive tsunami that struck in December 2004. *Jack Gruber/USA TODAY*

Sunrise in Krueng Raya, Indonesia.
Jack Gruber/USA TODAY

Page xi: (top row, from left) Steve Elfers/Army Times/USA TODAY, Tim Dillon/USA TODAY, Jym Wilson/USA TODAY, Jack Gruber/USA TODAY, Jack Gruber/USA TODAY; (second row, from left) Robert Deutsch/USA TODAY, Jack Gruber/USA TODAY, Robert Deutsch/USA TODAY, Tim Dillon/USA TODAY, Anne Ryan/USA TODAY; (third row, from left) Jack Gruber/USA TODAY, Greg L'Heureux/USA TODAY, Tim Dillon/USA TODAY, H. Darr Beiser/USA TODAY, Robert Hanashiro/USA TODAY; (fourth row, from left) M. Scott Mahaskey/Army Times/USA TODAY, Eileen Blass/USA TODAY, Jack Gruber/USA TODAY, Jack Gruber/USA TODAY, Jack Gruber/USA TODAY; (fifth row, from left) Robert Hanashiro/USA TODAY, Robert Hanashiro/USA TODAY, Jack Gruber/USA TODAY, Kathy Chu/USA TODAY, Jack Gruber/USA TODAY.

Pages 2-3: (top row, from left) Robert Giroux/Getty Images, USA TODAY, Robert Deutsch/USA TODAY, Tim Dillon/USA TODAY, Tim Dillon/USA TODAY, M. Scott Mahaskey/Army Times/USA TODAY, Kathleen Hennessy/USA TODAY; (second row, from left) Robert Hanashiro/USA TODAY, Jack Gruber/USA TODAY, H. Darr Beiser/USA TODAY, Roberto Schmidt/AFP/Getty Images, Robert Hanashiro/USA TODAY; (third row, from left) H. Darr Beiser/USA TODAY, Eileen Blass/USA TODAY, USA TODAY, AP Images, Tim Dillon/USA TODAY, H. Darr Beiser/USA TODAY.

Pages 110-111: (top row, from left) Jym Wilson/USA TODAY, Catherine Henriette/AFP/Getty Images, Barb Ries/USA TODAY, Jack Gruber/USA TODAY, AP Images; (second row, from left) Allan Tannenbaum/Time Life Pictures/Getty Images.

Pages 148-149: (top row, from left) Tim Dillon/USA TODAY, Jack Gruber/USA TODAY, Tim Dillon/USA TODAY, Jeff Haynes/AFP/Getty Images, Bob Riha Jr./USA TODAY, Jack Gruber/USA TODAY, Evan Siegle/USA TODAY; (second row, from left) H. Darr Beiser/USA TODAY, Frederik Balfour/AFP/Getty Images, Matthew Minard/Shreveport Times/USA TODAY, Robert Hanashiro/USA TODAY, USA TODAY, Justin Sullivan/Getty Images.

Pages 198-199: (top row, from left) Robert Deutsch/USA TODAY, H. Darr Beiser/USA TODAY, Robert Hanashiro/USA TODAY, Porter Binks/USA TODAY, Jason Lee/USA Today, Todd Plitt/USA TODAY, Robert Hanashiro/USA TODAY, Robert Hanashiro/USA TODAY, Robert Deutsch/USA TODAY; (second row, from left) H. Darr Beiser/USA TODAY, Kevin P. Casey/Bloomberg News/USA TODAY, Anne Ryan/USA TODAY, Eileen Blass/USA TODAY, Tim Dillon/USA TODAY, H. Darr Beiser/USA Today, Michael Schwarz/USA TODAY, Dixie Vereen/USA TODAY, Jack Gruber/USA TODAY.